Dear Hartley

Dear Hartley

THOUGHTS ON CHARACTER, KINDNESS, AND BUILDING A BRIGHTER WORLD

JEDEDIAH BILA

CENTER STREET

New York   Nashville

Center Street
Hachette Book Group
1290 Avenue of the Americas, New York, NY 10104
centerstreet.com
twitter.com/centerstreet

First Edition: November 2021

Center Street is a division of Hachette Book Group, Inc. The Center Street name and logo are trademarks of Hachette Book Group, Inc.

The publisher is not responsible for websites (or their content) that are not owned by the publisher.

Library of Congress Cataloging-in-Publication Data
Names: Bila, Jedediah, author.
Title: Dear Hartley : letters to my son / Jedediah Bila.
Description: First edition. | New York : Center Street, [2021] | Summary: "Jedediah Bila writes both honest, reflective letters to guide her son as he navigates through life, and a common-sense appeal to the next generation to drop the worst and take the best of what we've given them. For a long time, Jedediah Bila wasn't the kind of person who spoke her mind. Despite talking for a living on various hit television shows, she preferred to keep her private life private. Now, however, she believes she has a message that the world—particularly young conservatives in the United States—should hear. In Dear Hartley, Bila writes fifty-two carefully crafted letters to her son. Some of these letters are short, and some are long. All of them, however, are written in Jedediah's conversational, quick-witted, authentic, relatable prose, and directed to her son Hartley. The letters will cover a wide range of topics, leaving no stone unturned, and will include politics, culture, education, nostalgia, work, fitness, nutrition, the everyday, and the esoteric. Readers will find it easy to dip into the short reads and dig into the longer thought pieces, finding insight, humor, and inspiration along the way"—Provided by publisher.
Identifiers: LCCN 2021025397 | ISBN 9781546001034 (hardcover) | ISBN 9781546001423 (ebook)
Subjects: LCSH: Bila, Jedediah. | Television personalities—United States—Biography. | Mothers and sons—United States. | Sons—Conduct of life.
Classification: LCC PN1992.4.B53 A3 2021 | DDC 791.4502/8092 [B]—dc23
LC record available at https://lccn.loc.gov/2021025397

ISBNs: 9781546001034 (hardcover), 9781546001423 (ebook)

Printed in the United States of America

LSC-C

Printing 1, 2021

To the next generation and beyond—I believe in you.

Contents

CONTENTS

CONTENTS

Dear Hartley

A Future Built on Letters

THE SUN IS SETTING over the Verrazzano-Narrows Bridge and our house is quiet for the first time since I woke up fourteen hours ago. I have a pen in my hand. A real, live pen with a silver barrel, its narrow nib ready to deposit black ink onto thick, ivory matte stationery. There are no electronics in sight, and my thoughtful husband has left me to my own undistracted devices. I finally have a literary room of one's own.

No excuses.

The time has come for me to write the letters of a lifetime. Letters to my son, Hartley, the full-of-life, full-of-energy baby boy currently sleeping soundly in his crib, hopefully dreaming something wonderful. They will be letters about my mistakes, achievements, relationships, decisions, and my right and wrong turns. They will be about values, obstacles big and small, and how I hope the world can be for him and his whole generation.

Parenting can be challenging to the heart and mind. There are worries as to how well we're preparing our children for this great thing called life. Sometimes we feel like we can never do enough, that we need to be in two (or three or four) places at once, that we've not said or done the exact right thing. We all know there is no "exact right thing" to say or do, but that's hard to accept sometimes too. The thing is, it's such precious cargo we're dealing with, these lives we've created that are vulnerable and curious about the ways of the world. We want everything to go wonderfully well, if not close to perfect, for them. Perfect is an impossible goal, but we love these children so much that we dream of perfection for them nonetheless.

We are currently in the oddest of days. The world spins on an axis of us vs. them, yours vs. mine. Everyone is so busy trying to defend their position and confirm their worldview that we leave little room to hear anyone else speak, let alone sit down to read a well-written letter and leave ourselves open to the possibility of, yes, persuasion.

Throughout my television career, I've sat on several big platforms, well aware that division is a business model for many, and a successful one. It's not my business model, and never will be. My goal in these letters, and from any platform I'm blessed with today or tomorrow, is to invite everyone to talk with me, share with me, and learn with me. I'm opening up my life and my heart in these pages, with the hope that we can figure things out together for my child, your child, your grandchild, and beyond.

In this time of polarization, confusion, and frustration, I still believe there are many people out there hungry for healthy conversation, hopeful for an exchange of ideas that doesn't involve shouting down the "other side." I also believe we have a lot in common when it comes to our desire to take care of our children.

I'm writing these letters for my child, who I love more than I ever thought possible, hoping that they will be something he can turn to for laughter, wisdom, and direction as he grows into the person he wants to be.

I'm writing to reach a generation of young adults, as well as the parents, relatives, and friends guiding them on their journeys.

I'm writing to help uncover the core of what many of us feel inside about the world and one another. Though we each have our own unique life experiences, I'm betting that our stories, and the lessons we've learned, have a lot in common. I'm betting that we share many of the same dreams for the children in our lives.

I'm writing with the hope that these letters tug at the hearts and minds of those who think they see the world differently from "those people over there" and may have forgotten that emotions like happiness and sadness unite us all.

My hope is to remind us where we've been and where we can go, what we've overcome and what we can overcome.

Hope. It's so important. I love my son so much. I also love my country, and I believe in us all. Despite the divisive noise out there, underneath it all, we're just people. And that means something.

I also write this book with an inch of trepidation.

This is a book about secrets and raw emotions, with my child's name right there on the cover. I thought long and hard about whether to write something so personal related to him and put it out there in this moment, with so much outrage around us. I wondered if people would say nasty things about him for no reason at all, or maybe for the sole reason of taking a jab at me. I decided to step through that inch of fear and start writing, because with so much fury out there right now, maybe this is the perfect time for this book to reach hearts and heads. Plus, I couldn't possibly encourage my kid to be honest, bold, and brave if I wasn't able to do it myself.

I'm hopeful that those who read this book will receive it in the spirit it's offered, as the start of a conversation about what I think most mothers and fathers hope for: a world that is less divisive and more inviting, less angry and more filled with big smiles and big hearts. I hope it speaks to the things on which we can agree, like safe playgrounds, clean air and water, good health, great education, opportunities for all of our children, and freshly baked cookies that come out of the oven just right.

Like any mom, I want my child to have a fulfilling, well-rounded life: mentally, emotionally, physically, and spiritually. And like every mom, I have thoughts on each of these areas: head, heart, hand, and higher power. They are all here, in these pages, in my letters to Hartley. My mistakes are in here too because I want him to know that we all make mistakes, that it's okay to make mistakes if we learn from them, and that sometimes mistakes help us find a better path.

These letters speak to what I believe, what I know, and what I'm learning. They speak to what I've gotten wrong (a lot of things) and what I've gotten right (less things).

I hope these letters speak to you and your children.

I hope they inspire you to write letters of your own to the people you love.

Most of all, I hope they get us talking, really talking with each other, in ways that make us healthier, happier, and full of life.

Jedediah
NYC, November 2021

We Begin

Dear Hartley,

The summer before my senior year of college was a rocky one. I had the good fortune of being invited to join a summer study-abroad program in Madrid. At the time, I wanted to pursue a doctorate in Spanish literature, but the only way I could afford it was to earn a full fellowship. The program in Madrid would increase my chances significantly. But something happened before I left that changed everything.

Well, not everything, but enough.

I had been dating this guy for almost two years and was pretty crazy about him. Not as crazy in love as I would eventually be with your daddy, but as you'll see, there are sometimes a few romances along the way to finding The One. This man and I had very little in common on paper, but back then, we somehow made more sense to me than anything else. He was going to work abroad in South America at the same time I was heading overseas to study. In fact, we were both departing the same day. We unofficially officially kind of sort of broke up the night before we left.

But didn't.

This is the way of young romance sometimes.

I spent a lot of that first week in Madrid roaming the city, trying to bury my head in books, running laps on the outdoor campus track. I used to play love songs on repeat while I ran, then I'd run faster and faster, but no matter what I did, I couldn't shake a feeling of dread. I was lost, but it was more than that. Whatever journey I was on with that man, well, I wasn't ready for it to be over just yet.

I cried. A lot.

I ran. A lot.

I roamed the city at night. Nothing seemed to help.

And then one day, I wrote my best friend a letter.

I sealed it and sent it to New York. She wrote me back soon after. Letter after letter came and went, and I found myself smiling again. Truthfully, writing those letters didn't make me miss the guy any less. In some ways, writing about him made me miss him more. But putting my thoughts down on paper, embarking on that conversational journey with my friend, began to heal me. I started to feel a little less broken and a little more motivated to get out there, explore the city, and take photos of my surroundings.

And through my words to her, I figured out what I was going to do.

I was going to stick with the study-abroad program, go back to New York briefly when it was over, then head to South America to see if there was something in that relationship worth fighting for. Through our exchange of ideas, through those letters, I found direction. And that direction helped me to feel alive again.

That man didn't turn out to be my soul mate. In fact, that trip to South America was my first step in realizing that a page of my life was turning, and that he likely wasn't meant to continue into my next chapter. I wouldn't meet my soul mate, your daddy, for another fifteen years. Those letters I wrote to my best friend, though, were pivotal in helping me figure out my whole relationship with that man. Without them, I might never have discovered so much of myself and what I really wanted.

And so, here I am once again, on a letter-writing journey. This time, to you, Hartley. I'm not writing to tell you what to do, or to tell you how to live. Well, okay, maybe I am doing some of that. But I'm also writing with the hope that my words will guide you through your own journey, make you think, spare you some of my mistakes, and offer you strength as you navigate obstacles and opportunities. Maybe, if we're lucky, you will discover hidden treasures in these stories that will help you uncover treasures of your own.

The night you were born, I started a letter. It began like this:

Dear Hartley,

We had our first conversation today. I smiled and you made a little noise back. It was the most beautiful sound I had ever heard. I'm in love with you already.

I remember that you started crying and I nursed you. The next few days got a little crazy. Then the next few months were a real learning experience for your daddy and me. Then COVID-19 and a quarantine hit the world, and I never did get back to those letters—until now.

I have so much I want to say to you about life, love, family—I could go on. And I will.

I sit here tonight, after you've just gone to bed. Daddy put you in pajamas and I read *Good Night, Moon* to you twice because you love it so much. You've snuggled up in your crib on your side with your little hands close to your face. You sleep just like me. This is one of my favorite times of day, looking at you on the baby monitor, wondering what you're dreaming about.

Every day, I get to watch you make your way in this world. You're a robust toddler as I write this, full of curiosity and wonder, big energy and loud noises. You climb on everything and never stop moving. You're so strong, Hartley. And when you want something, you go get it with vigor, whether it's your red truck or some water from your little cup to recharge. I wonder how this will translate in later years and if you will be the kind of man who goes after what he wants. I hope so.

You're stubborn too. (Can't imagine where you got that from.) I can't make a meal for you unless it includes avocados. You love avocados. And applesauce. You had Mama making fresh guacamole and eating five apples a day when I was pregnant.

And you love Daisy, our four-pound Maltipoo. It's fascinating how you've become friends. You even manage to play tug-of-war with her tiny Frisbee. "Daisy" was your first full word.

You love Grandma and Grandpa's kitty cats too. What a big smile you give them when you see them. It's a gift to have a child who relates to animals so well and already sees how much they can teach us.

I'm crazy in love with you and every little thing you do. Of course, I know that "loving every little thing you do" may get more complicated as you grow. You'll start to break out into your own person, stretch the boundaries of your personality, test the limits with Daddy and me, and gather a crop of your own friends. I know I'll like some of them and worry that others could hurt you. We'll disagree on some things, maybe some pretty big things. And I know you'll need to broaden your world beyond us. I'm not quite ready for that yet, but I will be, and I'm excited for you and everything you will discover.

I want so much for you in life.

I hope you love with your whole heart.

I hope you pursue truth fearlessly and learn how to reason with your own mind.

I hope you're the type of person who people seek out for advice and trust with their hopes and fears.

Most of all, I want you to be happy and healthy.

So, I'm going to spend some days and nights writing these letters to you. Sharing how I feel about the world as it is now, in 2021, and how I hope it will be for you, and for all of us, in five years, ten years, twenty years, and beyond.

Every night, before I lay you down in your crib, I say six very special words to you: "I love you more than life." I say them because I love the gift of life so much, and yet I love you even more than that. I will be closing each of these letters with those six special words, just to make sure you never forget...

I love you more than life,
Mama

Unexpected Journeys

Dear Hartley,

For a long time, I didn't know I wanted a baby. I would see moms with their kids in supermarkets, malls, or doctors' offices and think, *That's just not me.* I didn't know why, but I just couldn't relate. In college, some of my friends would talk about marriage and kids. I would instead envision a one-bedroom apartment in Manhattan and a job I loved. I couldn't see the family portrait for some reason. The thought of having a child also scared me a little. Okay, a lot. *Could I handle a baby? Would my own life disappear?*

In my twenties, I got a graduate degree and worked a lot of different jobs trying to find what I loved, or trying to find myself, or a little of both. It wasn't until I met your daddy that everything changed...and even then, it didn't change for me right away.

The first time I went out with Daddy, we hit a burger joint. We were just friends, out for a night of good conversation. I remember him telling me that he wanted a kid and a garage and fun car pools to soccer practices on weekends.

Car pools? I thought. *For real?* Who was this guy?

I guess I wasn't as ready for those things as your daddy was, which is funny because he's younger than I am. But as the weeks and months progressed, I started to see things differently. Slowly at first, then more quickly. I started to love him so much that I began to imagine what a little version of us would look like and how amazing it would be to see that little person smile with Daddy's lips or my eyes. And so, the idea of you was born, and for the first time in my life, it didn't scare me. It made me smile.

Having you inside my belly was surreal. Although I felt totally in sync with your hunger and thirst, we didn't always align in some other areas.

When I moved, you were still. When I was still, you moved.

You hated my early bedtimes the nights before work.

When I'd sit down to watch a movie, you'd kick forcefully, nudging me to walk around. When I was at the gym getting some exercise, you were at total peace. You loved motion.

You also hated the sound of the sonogram machine. We could see you putting your little hand up, as if to say: *Talk to the hand.* It was clear that you wanted to be left alone. Yep, you were definitely my child.

Even though we spent so much time together when I was pregnant, I had no idea what it would mean to finally see you face-to-face. That first moment we met, when you looked right up at me, was wild. *Did that little person just come out of my body? Wow.* Forget Jerry Maguire, you had me before hello.

Your first smile, your first laugh, the first time you hugged me, all left me feeling like I'd found a part of myself I had buried.

My first Mother's Day was wonderful. *I'm someone's mama,* I kept saying.

I sometimes still can't believe it. I tell you I love you about ten thousand times a day. You can't say "Mom, stop smothering me" yet, so I win, for now. By the time you read this, you won't be so little anymore, and I imagine I'll probably have to sneak my way into a hug and a kiss, but I hope not. And I hope that you'll always know how much I love you, that I'd move mountains for you. I'll never forget, even for one millisecond, how lucky I am to be your mama, and how much I've learned from loving you.

No doubt, this is what moms have been feeling since the beginning of time, all over the world. It's a crazy kind of love. The source of Greek tragedies and countless Lifetime TV epic family dramas. Grandma used to say to me, "We shared a heartbeat once." I'd roll my eyes as a kid in a "Here goes Mom again" kind of way. But I get it now. It's like I knew you before you even got here. How incredible is that?

I have always lived my life footloose and fancy-free. Skydiving, roller coasters, pretty much every daredevil activity was mine for the taking. Since becoming your mama, my thought process on those things is a little more complicated. That's not to say I won't do them, but there's always this part of my brain that thinks of you first and how it could impact you. Even when Daddy and I got sick with COVID in 2020, our focus immediately went to you. We were consumed with making sure you'd be okay.

Before I had you, I thought it would drive me crazy to be consumed by another person like this. I thought I'd lose myself. As it turns out, it's kind of great. All the petty stuff of life falls away, and in having a child, you sometimes *find* yourself.

You've taught me so much about life already. You laugh at the craziest of times, which reminds me to do so. You find joy in the simplest of objects. You take the time to notice the leaves, trees, and flowers outside, and never just pass them by. You have managed to get my priorities in order faster than anyone else ever could.

I thought that having a child was going to be all about you learning from me. I found out quickly that a big part of being your mama is me learning from you. Having a baby changed me in all the best ways. If you have a child of your own one day, I hope they do for your life what you have already done for mine. I'm so excited for all of the lessons we'll learn from each other.

Having you has been a beautiful unexpected journey.

In life, the unexpected journeys are often the best kind. They bring you gifts you never even knew you wanted, gifts for which you wind up being so grateful.

Embrace the unexpected, Hartley. The unexpected moments. The unexpected choices, paths, and people. Don't let them scare you.

And thank you, my child, for the many wonderful surprises you've already given me.

I love you more than life,
Mama

Beware of the Bright Orange Hoodie

Dear Hartley,

I remember getting ready for that summer study-abroad trip to Madrid I mentioned earlier. Packing for seven weeks proved to be a lot harder than I thought. Grandma kept coming into my room to beg me to take a jacket. Or several.

It was summer. *A jacket? Why?* I knew that Spain would be super hot.

"I'm telling you, take something warm. You'll need it for the plane, the restaurants. You're going to get cold."

I heard what she was saying, but her words sort of went in one ear and out the other.

I finished packing all of the things I knew I'd need for Spain in the summer: shorts, T-shirts, dresses, and way too many pairs of sandals. Neither a jacket nor a sweater was in the mix.

Grandma and Grandpa took me to the airport to see me off.

"Did you bring a jacket?" Grandma asked me at the gate.

I shook my head no and gestured around to all of the nearby

passengers in tank tops and shorts. She took off the oversized, bright orange hoodie she had wrapped around her waist. "I'm telling you, you're going to need this." Reluctantly, I took it, mostly to get her to stop talking about it, and stuffed it into my carry-on bag, annoyed to have the extra bulk. I figured I could just leave it behind somewhere and no one (i.e., Grandma) would be the wiser.

I got on the plane and tucked into my window seat. The excitement and anxiety of going on a big trip surged through me as we took off into the wild blue yonder over JFK Airport.

"We've reached our flying altitude of thirty thousand feet," the pilot announced, and I got myself comfortable for the next five hours of quiet, reading, movies, and contemplation.

Only, the thing was, I couldn't settle in.

Something wasn't quite right.

Oh, yeah, that was it—it was roughly negative 60 degrees in the giant metal container we were flying in.

I was freezing. And I mean *freezing*.

I retrieved the hoodie from my bag, put it on, and was warm and cozy for the rest of the trip.

I soon discovered that a lot of the places I would go in Madrid would have their air-conditioning on full blast. It also got quite cool at night, especially when we traveled to the south of Spain by the water. Did I have my favorite denim jacket? Or the retro tie-dyed blazer I loved? Or the super soft cardigan I'd bought at my favorite store? Nope. I had been stubborn, didn't listen to your grandma, and as a result, had nothing warm except her oversized, bright orange hoodie to wear with, well, everything. Fast-forward to me in a club wearing a dress and…the orange hoodie. A fancy restaurant in a jumpsuit and…the orange hoodie. Museums. Lounges. Walks at night. The oversized orange hoodie was there for it all.

These days, I don't get on a plane or enter a movie theater without a sweatshirt or jacket in hand. In fact, if I tell Grandma I'm going anywhere indoors in the summer, I can always rely on her to say:

"Do you have a jacket? It's going to be cold…"

And I do.

Bottom line: Life gets cold. Don't get trapped with nothing warm to wear except an oversized, bright orange hoodie.

I love you more than life,

Mama

Life Is Not a Straight Line (into the Beautifully Unfamiliar)

Dear Hartley,

There's a saying, sometimes attributed to George Eliot, that I totally love:

"It is never too late to be what you might have been."

Never too late. Remember that.

Gosh, Hartley, I have changed my mind about so many things. And have jumped from one life path to another several times. Thank heavens for some of those pivots.

The first significant time I changed paths was when I shifted my initial career choice. I'd received a full fellowship to Columbia University for their PhD program in Spanish literature. Intent on embarking on several years of study, research, and a career in academia, I quickly realized that the place, the work, and the path weren't for me. I left with a master's in hand to find a journey that felt right.

The second significant time I changed my mind was when I went to work for an insurance company, thinking that maybe I'd surprise myself and like corporate America. I was working Downtown across the street from the World Trade Center. Terrorist-hijacked airplanes hit the Trade Center towers on September 11, 2001, and I ran for my life through the streets of Manhattan. When I later found out that I was supposed to be in a meeting in one of those towers early that morning, and had accidentally missed the memo telling me to be there, my world shifted. My mind shifted. Everyone in that meeting had died. I could barely process that. I grieved, worked my way through the shock, and decided that I would never spend another day doing anything I didn't want to do.

I soon realized that life wasn't always that simple. So I added this to my thinking: If I ever got stuck on a path that wasn't right for me, stuck for reasons beyond my control, I'd begin paving a new path while there, readying myself for a leap. See, even my advice to myself took a necessary pivot.

A few months after September 11, 2001, I left that stable insurance company job to find meaning in life, which I somehow found while busting my butt waiting tables in a two-story lounge from 9:00 p.m. to 4:00 a.m. I also took some acting classes and ventured briefly to Los Angeles with the acting bug. (I should've stayed in L.A. a little longer. That's an example of how I changed my mind too soon.)

The fourth big time I jumped lanes was after I took a few teaching jobs, first at a college, then at a Catholic school on Staten Island, then at a private high school in Manhattan. Though I enjoyed aspects of the work and loved the kids, it wasn't my calling. I started writing, which always has a funny way of helping me find my focus, got offers to appear on television due to my writing, and quit teaching to enter the land of TV.

The fifth significant time I changed my mind was when I thought for sure marriage wasn't for me. Then I met your daddy and thought,

Hmm, maybe I was wrong about this whole life partner thing. I was late to the party on marriage, but your daddy was worth the wait.

The sixth hilarious time I changed my mind was when I decided to have a traditional wedding. I'd always told your grandma that if I was going to get married at all, the wedding was going to be by the ocean, with me in combat boots and denim, and a handful of guests. Maybe we'd play beach volleyball afterward or have a cookout. I told your grandpa that maybe I'd get married on a roller coaster. That was a bit of a stretch, but I love roller coasters so much that I figured it would be a guaranteed good time. Your mama is a casual, no-frills kind of gal. Well, most of the time.

Lo and behold, your daddy and I wound up getting married in a fairy-tale ceremony in the exquisite library of a castle, in front of dozens of people. My wedding planner, Michael, had taken us to the castle on an "It doesn't hurt to look" journey. I fell in love with that castle when I saw its library. It looked just like a library you'd see in your favorite old movie, complete with old books and old paintings and old lighting fixtures. I even walked down the aisle in... wait for it... a dress. And not just any dress, but a ball gown that looked like it was right out of the old movie the library was from. Michael hadn't been big on my denim shorts and T-shirt idea, so he had taken me to a store on another "It doesn't hurt to look" journey, with a "Just try some on for me" plea. I bought the first dress I tried on, a lace strapless gown with a train. That was after I had told Michael in the car on the way there, "No lace, no strapless, no trains." Michael was an angel for putting up with me.

We now have pictures of your daddy and me running around in the snow at that castle, me in my ball gown with Daddy's tuxedo jacket over it. It was the most perfect winter wonderland wedding. I was so afraid that a traditional wedding wouldn't be me, but we fixed that by making it our own. I had snowball fights on the outdoor lawn in my gown, which is exactly what anyone who knows me would expect. Daddy and I even built a wedding snowman, bow tie included.

The seventh big time I changed my mind was when I thought I didn't want kids. I fell in love with your daddy, something in the universe shifted, and I knew that there was a baby out there waiting to be ours. Now I have you, my little buddy, my partner in crime.

I've made some good choices and I've made some bad ones. There were a lot of disappointments and wrong turns along the way. Regardless of the paths I chose, I knew that I was comfortable changing my mind, comfortable moving out of bad energy and into good, comfortable dropping the reliable for the unpredictable when the reliable no longer made sense.

I was okay with being guided by my inner voice.

Don't be afraid to change your mind, Hartley. Sometimes things feel good right now and not good later. When they stop feeling good, make changes. I'm not telling you to abandon tough situations in hard times. That's not my message here at all. Relationships, for example, get hard. There are challenges, many of them. People who love each other and respect each other can often get through those challenges together, and often come out stronger and more bonded to each other on the other side. What I'm talking about are life paths that drain your soul in a negative way and leave you feeling dark, people who say bad things to you, and workplaces that disrespect you or devalue your contributions. When faced with circumstances like those, don't feel stuck. Consider a new path that inspires you, even if that new path has some obstacles and challenges of its own.

Never be afraid to upset the status quo when the status quo is no longer healthy. It is never too late to tread into the beautifully unfamiliar.

And remember, life is complex. Sometimes we make a good change, then get lost on a journey that doesn't feel good, then make another good change, then get lost again. Life is a process and that's okay. After 9/11, I made a promise to myself to change paths, and I kept that promise. But that change wasn't the be-all, end-all discovery of my life. Twenty years later, after COVID happened, I was reminded yet again of the fragility of life. I made myself a promise similar to the one I had made two decades earlier: to follow my heart and my passion, to remember who I am and what I want to bring to this world. We don't always follow our own advice perfectly or all at once, and sometimes we discover reminders in both pleasant and unpleasant circumstances that shout: *"Remember who you are."* Wake-up calls. And so, we listen again and try to do better for ourselves this time around.

I hope you'll grow to be in touch with your body and your mind, and their relationship to each other. They'll help you figure out when dark situations get too dark, when it's time to make a move.

I hope you're excited by new journeys and new paths, even though they can be a little scary and a lot unpredictable.

I hope you prioritize the things you love, and that if you ever lose sight of them, you find a way to get back on track, with the knowledge that it is never too late to turn what you love into your job, your hobby, your escape, your source of income—any and all of it.

It's never too late to open yourself up to what suddenly feels amazing.

I love you more than life,
Mama

Living the Dream

Dear Hartley,

People read, write, and talk about the American dream a lot. Like many people, I feel like I've lived a taste of it.

I grew up in a small condo behind the Staten Island Mall. It was a charming two-and-a-half-bedroom space decorated like an adorable, cozy cottage. Grandma decorates everything beautifully, and it had that winter getaway kind of feel, complete with a fireplace and real brick wall. Grandma and Grandpa worked hard to pay off that condo's mortgage and saved up to send me to one of the best K–12 schools on the Island. Money didn't come easy, but Grandma and Grandpa always put me first, so I didn't want for things like trendy boots for my birthday or that cool ruffle top for the seventh-grade dance. I worked hard in school to get scholarships to college and grad school, and Grandma and Grandpa covered every expense they could and more. I knew that we didn't live in a giant house like some of my classmates, and that we had to save up for nice vacations or a new car lease, but it wasn't until years later that I realized the sacrifices they had made for me, sometimes big ones. What a gift to have parents like that.

Last year, I revisited that condo I grew up in. It's a dark brown, two-story brick-and-wood structure, in a line of similar, connected condos at the end of a cul-de-sac. I walked around outside and even thought about knocking on the front door, but figured the people who lived there would think I was nuts. I thought about a lot as I looked up at my old bedroom window. Somehow the girl who grew up in a quaint condo behind the Staten Island Mall had landed on television. What a country.

My parents worked really hard, and so did I. I used to get up at 4:30 in the morning to study when I was in high school. I worked my butt off in college. But still, what would all of that have meant in a country without opportunity? Without the chance to shape your future with hard work and personal drive?

I'm not saying that some people don't have more financial and familial challenges than others, or that some aren't more privileged than others. Of course, that's all true. Some people's starts in life are just plain easier, as are their paths along the way. Admitting that is just honest. But the thing is that in America, we all have a chance, some chance, to get where we want to go. Ambition, hard work, commitment to a task—these things are all valued here and can shift your life in big ways, regardless of what your starting point looked like.

I believe in many of the values that built the United States and encouraged its citizens to cultivate a strong sense of independence. I believe in the responsibility your dad and I have to construct a strong foundation of love, kindness, and confidence from which you can build a life of conviction, empathy, and accountability. We are all so lucky to live here, to grow here, in this nation like no other. But we are also facing some very real challenges as a nation today.

Our country is so divided politically. Social media highlights and feeds those divisions even more. Unfortunately, what I see too often are people eager for total agreement all the time and for spaces without dissent, people craving echo chambers instead of challenges to their way of thinking, people ready to jump down the throats of those who dare to offer a different point of view. Mediums preaching to their own choirs are all too common. Where once there were schools for encouraging free thinking, there are now institutions that perpetually march toward one way of seeing the world. I see students less likely to think for themselves, less encouraged to do so, and sometimes afraid to cultivate ideas deemed outside the teacher-approved way of thinking.

Now is the time to fix these mistakes, first by recognizing them, then by moving forward with bold determination to do better, for all of us. We've all had different life experiences and different struggles. So have our parents, grandparents, great-grandparents, and beyond. The key to doing better as a nation is to get to a place where we know better, and we all get to *that* place by listening to one another and surrounding ourselves with a variety of voices eager to share and hear life stories. Robust debate in shared forums is essential. We need to at least try to walk in each other's shoes, to see where someone else is coming from and where they've been, to understand what shaped a different worldview. We need to allow ourselves to be challenged and consider that someone else, every now and then, may be right.

You can be part of a generation that takes care of themselves and one another, respects one another, and values sincere conversations that lift every boat with the rising tide. You can be that friend who listens to someone's very different life experience and learns something amazing from it that you can then share with the world. You can be that teacher who welcomes hearty debate in the classroom or that student who engages in the kind of sincere, respectful discussion that builds great nations. If and when your country feels like it's losing its way, I hope that you question why, and have challenging conversations about how to make it better. And when it's time to critique mistakes of the past, remember that no nation should be exempt from that critique, as no nation is perfect, and we are only as strong as our willingness to admit our mistakes. I hope that ideals like freedom and opportunity will ring loudly in your heart, head, and voice.

While dressing you on your first Fourth of July, I remember thinking that I wanted four very specific freedoms for you.

The freedom:

to love,
to be,
to learn, and
to discover.

I believe that you and your generation have the power to really change things. Many people fought so hard for this country. They wrote a Declaration of Independence and a Constitution and gave us a beautiful start toward growth. Those people weren't perfect, and the documents weren't perfect either, but it was a beginning.

A hopeful beginning.

We must take care of our country, Hartley. And in order to do so, we must take care of one another. I hope that you'll play a role in all this, with lots of heart, compassion, and strength. I want the American dream I've tasted to be preserved for you and your whole generation. Because I can't imagine where I'd be without a country in which so many amazing things are possible.

I love you more than life,
Mama

The Art & Craft of Conversation

Dear Hartley,

Your grandma, grandpa, daddy, and I recently got into a great discussion. We were outside on the first warm afternoon of the year, seated at a big table, sharing some pre-dinner snacks. The conversation started with a TV show, led to a discussion about culture, and ended with talking about family. At times, it was passionate. At others, full of laughs. As the conversation buzzed, each person sharing a thought and reacting, your eyes followed us closely, darting from voice to voice. You were only a toddler, but you were really listening. When someone got serious, you lasered in on them with curious eyes. When we laughed, you laughed. I knew that if you had the capacity to form and share your opinions, you would have done so. I can't wait for that day.

We make it a point to include you in these conversations. Daddy and I want to ensure that you know, from the start, how to be comfortable in a setting with different points of view. I grew up like this, enjoying dinners at my Nanny and Poppy's apartment with Nanny's siblings. She was the oldest of thirteen kids, so I was immediately exposed to a baker's dozen–plus of perspectives. The chatter was noisy, the food delicious, the love abundant, and I ate it all up.

For the most part, I sat and listened back then, like you do now. I wasn't always so ready to share my thoughts with the world. I was a shy kid. Super shy, actually, which might surprise those who see me passionately voicing my thoughts on television. When I was in the first grade, my teacher called Grandma to ask if I could talk.

"Yes, I assure you, she talks plenty at home," Grandma replied.

I guess you could say I was just taking it all in back then, that I wasn't quite ready to share what was on my mind with the outside world.

In high school, things changed. I had this teacher, this super smart teacher, who seemed to know everything. And I mean *everything*. It was incredible. She was a walking historical encyclopedia. But she wasn't just a vessel of facts, she was also committed to helping us grow into independent adults, and that included teaching us how to debate and defend our views. It was there, in that freshman Global Studies classroom, that I found my voice. Years later, I discovered that my teacher's personal views were often different from mine. What a great testament to her teaching that I never knew that back then. She taught us how to logically present the best version of our views and ourselves. I have been trying my best to do that ever since.

I have plenty of opinions on just about everything.

Health and wellness: Exercise, yes. Good nutrition, yes. Giving yourself anxiety about either, no.

Culture: Freedom, yes. Repression, no.

Lifestyle: Music with lyrics, yes. Nineties television, yes. Nature and outdoors, yes. Esports, no.

Fashion: Comfortable, yes. Uncomfortable, no.

Politics: Points of view, yes. Independent thinking, yes. Political parties and entrenched positions for position's sake, no.

I believe in debate and discussion. So even my "no's" above are open to being convinced. Tell me why you disagree, and I'll tell you what I think about what you said, and maybe we'll figure some things out together. When people on divergent paths of thought connect on an issue, it can yield an incredible moment of growth for everyone. After I've spoken with someone, or had an exchange of ideas on television, I want everyone who was involved in the discussion to feel optimistic and heard. I want us all to feel like we've had our eyes opened in some way and that we've channeled something positive, not negative, into the world around us.

Anger drains the soul and taxes the bodies we live in. I don't thrive on that energy. I thrive on listening, laughter, and open minds. Positive emotions feed our precious immune systems. Good conversations should excite our brains and awaken uplifting feelings, even when we find ourselves disagreeing on this or that. Most importantly, good conversations should make us stretch out of our comfort zones and grow into better people.

Too many people no longer want to have a real conversation. Instead, they want to hit their talking points and state their fixed position again and again. I see this on both sides of many equations: politically, economically, culturally. And that's too bad, because it's a loss for everyone. It's the loss of a chance to learn and grow, to connect, to challenge yourself and figure out if you really feel the way you think you feel.

My approach to conversation and hot-button issues is pretty simple. I'm a think-for-myself kind of gal. I don't like talking points or fixed allegiances to political parties and politicians. Because of that, my opinions can be unpredictable, which is exactly how it should be if we're free-thinking people. I believe in holding people accountable for bad behavior and taking responsibility for our own actions, words, and choices.

I believe in speaking your mind honestly, regardless of the audience you're engaging.

I'm also a pretty nostalgic kind of gal. I dream of a world where people have long conversations in person, on walks through nature, like Ralph Waldo Emerson, Louisa May Alcott, and Henry David Thoreau once did. There's so much happening in the world right now that's worth talking about. There are many challenges that can be met only if we listen and learn from one another. I want to do all of that, Hartley. I want to hear from people who feel differently from me. I want to try to understand why.

This afternoon, when it was raining outside and growing dark, you and I spent some time together in the kitchen. We sat in our cozy sweats, enjoying the oatmeal cookies we had baked from scratch.

Those are my favorite times. You and me and our special chats. I talk and you listen. You babble and I listen. It's all some kind of wonderful.

My wish for you and your generation is that you pay attention to how you feel, express it to others, and listen to them express their feelings back. My hope is that you'll be the generation that learns about themselves by listening to the journeys of others. I hope you'll be the children who can handle different points of view and the adults who can make your case without throwing your hands up in angst when others disagree.

Sometimes, Hartley, on those rainy afternoons like we had today, we just sit quietly and look out the window for a few moments. Silence can be a conversation of its own, filling a room with the energy people feel toward each other. Sometimes silence can speak louder than words in many different ways.

There will be people in your life who you feel you can really talk to. I hope I'm one of them. Treasure all of those people, Hartley. So much of the world's heartache could be fixed if we could just remember how to talk things through.

I love you more than life,
Mama

Jumping to Assumptions

Dear Hartley,

When I was in middle school, a classmate invited me to her birthday party. Let's call her Chelsea. I was really, really shy, but so excited to be invited. Grandma even let me pick out what I was going to wear and helped me do my hair. I remember that I had bought Chelsea a white denim jacket with little fringes on the sleeves and Grandma wrapped it in silver sparkly wrapping paper. As we approached the driveway of her house, I looked up and got nervous. Her house was so big. It was the most beautiful house I had ever seen. I'll never forget it, a big white mansion with two tall white columns in the front, black shutters on all the windows, and a large circular driveway. I opened the car door and adjusted my button-down shirt and jeans. *Am I dressed nice enough? Did I buy her a nice enough gift?*

I knocked on the door and a nice lady greeted us. She was wearing what looked like a uniform. I later found out she was in charge of taking care of Chelsea when her parents were at work. She also cooked the meals and had made us a delicious lunch of homemade pizzas, baked ziti, finger sandwiches, and too many desserts to fit on one table. The chocolate cake was to die for.

At one point, I had to go to the bathroom and got lost. The house really was that big. Chelsea's dad was a doctor and her mom did something with numbers and banking that I can't remember. Their basement looked like something out of a movie with a full dance floor, a disco ball, two pool tables, a full bar and lounge area, and a separate room with loads of arcade games.

I had a great time that day. I made some new friends and even swam in their heated swimming pool. Chelsea lent me one of her swimsuits, and she had nine or ten giant pool floats, one for each of us. I was shy, but I really liked Chelsea. And she seemed to like me too. It was nice to make a new friend.

"Maybe I can come to your house next time," she said as I left.

"Yeah, that would be—" I froze.

Something gurgled in the pit of my stomach.

"—great," I managed to finish.

Chelsea smiled and waved goodbye.

As Grandma drove me home that day, I was more quiet than usual. I was stuck in my head. This unfortunate pattern of mulling things over (and over and over) would continue until, well, now. Even though I loved our house, our fireplace, and my bedroom that Grandma had made bigger by knocking down the wall between my room and a small home office, our house suddenly felt so small compared to Chelsea's. *If she came over, would she be disappointed? Would she not like me because I didn't have an arcade or a dance floor? Would she find it too easy to find the bathroom? Would she not want to be my friend if I didn't live in a house like hers?*

My mind was whirling.

Ultimately, I invited Chelsea to my house about a month later. I was still anxious about it, but I also wanted to hang out with my new friend. Grandma cooked spaghetti and meatballs and served Italian pastries from our favorite pastry shop. Chelsea said it was the best meal she had ever eaten. Later, we went to our condominium's community pool and Grandma packed potato and egg sandwiches on Italian bread for a snack. Chelsea said she had never eaten those before, but she loved them. We laughed, swam, and even played some tennis on the community courts.

"Your mom is the coolest mom ever," she said while we ate ice pops on our little deck. "I love this house and don't want to leave!"

My face lit up. I loved my house too. And I started to feel silly for having worried that she wouldn't.

I had made so many assumptions about Chelsea. I had assumed that because she had more money than I did, she might not want to be my friend. I had assumed that she might frown upon a house that was way smaller than hers. I had assumed that she'd be bored without a game room or a dance floor, that she wouldn't want to swim in a community pool after spending so much time in a giant heated pool of her own.

As it turned out, Chelsea wasn't like that at all. She didn't judge me or compare my house to hers. She didn't seem to think anything about the differences between our lives that I had spent so much time focusing on. It wasn't fair to her that I had made those assumptions. And I hadn't been fair to myself either, assuming that the size of my house would somehow be more important to her than the kind of friend I would be.

The thing about assumptions, Hartley, is that they're often wrong. Sometimes they reflect insecurities we have about our appearances or other parts of our lives, which we then assume someone else is going to care about. But even when we know how wrong they can be, assumptions happen all the time. It's part of human nature to assume, and it takes work to grow out of that reflex to assume x, y, or z about someone.

People have assumed a lot of stuff about me. They've made assumptions because I grew up in Staten Island, because I worked at Fox News, because I co-hosted *The View*, because I married someone younger than I am. It's absurd. When people make assumptions, they don't allow me to simply be who I was, who I am, who I become.

Brace yourself, Hartley, for people to make a lot of assumptions about you too. They might assume how much money you have, or don't have, based on the neighborhood you live in, what type of person you are based on the clothes you wear and the car you drive, who you'd vote for based on the lifestyle you live, or what you value based on the school you went to. People may also make assumptions about you because I'm your mama and have a very public record of my opinions and jobs. Sometimes they will be right, or within the range of right. But many, many times, they will be wrong.

Assumptions are just plain silly. More than that, they're lazy.

They can also be incredibly unkind to you and to others.

Think before you assume things about others. Think about how you wouldn't want them assuming things about you. Think about all you stand to gain by meeting someone and, without making any assumptions, letting them show you who they are.

I love you more than life,
Mama

Fitted Sheets

Dear Hartley,

I still can't fold a fitted sheet properly.

One day, you'll be all grown up in your own apartment, doing your own laundry. You'll take fresh sheets out of the dryer and begin folding them. I warn you in advance that you may lose a portion of your sanity and break a substantial sweat trying to get that fitted sheet into some semblance of order.

I'm here to tell you it's not worth the angst.

Few people can fold those darn things well, if at all. Your grandma is one of those people who can. In addition to wrapping presents like a professional gift wrapper (I swear, you can't even see the tape), she can somehow fold a fitted sheet into a perfect little square. It almost looks ironed. Mama's folded fitted sheet, on the other hand, pokes out of the closet like a ball of organic cotton trying to break free, corners exposed and wrinkles throughout. (As a side note, my wrapped gifts also feature plenty of visible tape, and the paper never quite lines up as it should.)

Life is short, Hartley. Don't let the fitted sheet get you down. You have my full permission to fold it up as quickly as possible and toss it in the closet looking like it needs a makeover.

Or you can ask Grandma for help. I still can't seem to get it right even with her help, but you may do better than I've done.

PS—I also give you full permission to stick anything you ever buy for me in a gift bag to avoid Scotch tape.

I love you more than life,
Mama

Home of the Brave

Dear Hartley,

During the COVID-19 pandemic, I bought you a long-sleeved T-shirt that read "Be Brave." It was the perfect shirt for you for two reasons. First, you were such a brave little guy when we all got COVID. And second, "Be brave" was a great message to send to the world, and I couldn't think of anyone better to share it than my little guy.

Too often, when we are afraid, we find ourselves stuck in that negative feeling, paralyzed by the fright, unable to face the source of it or escape from it. Sometimes fear is the result of small things you encounter in life that you can talk through with family or friends. Other times, fear is prompted by a very real event that comes upon you suddenly and takes hard work to overcome.

Brave people don't deny fear. As the saying goes: courage isn't lacking fear, it's having the fortitude to face it.

It's okay to acknowledge being afraid. Fear is a very real emotion and there will be moments in life when you'll be scared. You've had some of those moments already. The thing is, when you face that fear, when you're honest about what you're feeling and why you're feeling it, you have a good chance of coming out stronger on the other side.

In 2020, a big fear of mine was realized. You, at the fragile age of four and a half months, got COVID. And worse, you got it from me.

The year 2020 was a strange time for our family and friends, our neighbors, the nation, and the world. COVID-19 went from being something no one knew anything about to something that was affecting almost everyone in every corner of the globe. We may have been separated by miles, oceans, or seas, but suddenly, we were all locked in the same conversation, one that involved a deadly virus, how it was spreading, what to do about it, and who was most at risk for serious illness, or worse.

You'll read plenty about COVID-19 in history books. You won't remember living that experience in our small one-bedroom Manhattan apartment, but that story will be right here for you to read. Because an important lesson for us all came out of that struggle. Let's start at the beginning...

COVID-19 was first seen in humans at the end of 2019, just around the time you were born. You arrived on this planet early one November morning that year. Mama took about three and a half months off from work to be close to you, and Daddy strung together his paternity leave, vacation days, and unused sick days to have as much time with you as possible. At about that time, awareness of COVID-19 was just emerging. At first, journalists were talking about the disease in Asia. Then it spread to Europe. In January, there were cases reported in the United States.

By the time February rolled around, I was nearing my return to work from maternity leave. The idea of going back was really hard for me because I knew I would miss you so much. We had been attached for more than three months (more than twelve months if you count pregnancy) and I loved having all of that time with you. Sure, there were a lot of sleepless nights, and breastfeeding had initially been tricky, but holding you in my arms felt more wonderful than anything I could have ever imagined.

The silver lining of returning to work was that my weekend job was filled with many ways to de-stress, recharge, and have some fun. *Fox & Friends Weekend* had typically been a pretty fun place to be, with lots of indoor and outdoor segments involving food, fitness, exotic animals, and exciting competitions with the guys. I had so many ideas for segments we could do, starting with a sledding competition and a nutrition segment I had been dreaming up for months.

I realized quickly upon my return that things had changed. The world had changed. The rapidly developing story of COVID-19 had taken over our show, and many other shows. This was how it needed to be. I understood that and had to figure out a way to shift my mind from maternity leave and brainstorming fitness segments to all-consuming COVID-19 content.

I was struggling with that a little. Okay, a lot. But I knew I had a very important job to do. I would be delivering information on national television about a deadly virus that was sweeping across the globe. People would be looking to me for guidance, and I couldn't disappoint them. I felt an obligation to get the facts straight, as well as to get them out there as soon as possible to help keep people safe.

Research is a big part of my approach to news and opinion, and I delved deeply into everything about the virus. I learned about how quickly it was spreading, the debilitating effects it was having on some people, and the deaths, the many devastating deaths. In order to do my job properly, I had to read up on COVID-19 constantly. My waking hours were consumed with facts and figures about a disease with many unknowns that was destroying so many families. It was tough energy for me to carry around all day, every day, without much of a break. I wasn't able to sleep well, my mind was racing a lot, and life felt heavy. But my biggest challenge was that I had this little baby at home to keep safe, and so much of what I was reading made me worry about you. *How would I protect you? What if I couldn't?*

I was scared.

Around mid-March, it got more intense. I was intent on covering the latest in discoveries, developments, and preparedness. I also had a lot to say about health and wellness as it related to COVID-19 and any virus, about comorbidities and what people could do, if anything, that was within their control. I wanted to hit the message home that while we don't always have control over what our bodies encounter in life (a virus, a bacteria, an insect bite), we often have some control over how our bodies react to those encounters.

We were interviewing doctors in person. Viewers shared their questions via email. Doctors didn't always have the answers because we were all learning about this virus day to day. There was a lot of "I don't know." That wasn't anyone's fault. That's just the way it is when something new comes on the scene so suddenly. The more research and information we gathered, the more I realized how unsure everyone was. Not just doctors, but also scientists and government officials. There was conflicting medical advice at every turn about what exactly was safe and which guidelines were optimal.

By the weekend of March 21, we stopped doing in-person interviews and began exercising a term that was new to us back then, but was soon to be everywhere:

We were "social distancing" in the studio.

Social distancing. I'm so sad to think that you were born into a world where that term soon became our norm, but it was something we had to do to protect ourselves and one another. It breaks my heart that so much of your first sixteen months of life existed in and around our home, with a few select family members, some small outdoor gatherings with friends, and very little interaction with other children. Believe me, I worried plenty about all of that too. What would it mean for your development to not have mommy-and-me playdates or daddy-and-me swim lessons? What would it do to you to see so many faces in masks all the time? Would you be more afraid at doctors' appointments if you couldn't get reassurance from their smiles? What would all of this do to children everywhere?

But this was reality and it seemed unavoidable.

February 29, 2020, I returned to work full-time and in the studio.

March 14, we were still on set, seated in the normal way we had always been.

Then, by March 21, we were positioned in separate areas of the studio. Guests were now remote.

The *Fox & Friends* camera crew was wonderful, doing everything they could to make our show run as smoothly as possible in such never-before-lived circumstances. By the way, Hartley, if you ever want to meet some of the hardest-working people in show business, get to know the crew of a television show. I've had the honor of working on several shows now, and the behind-the-scenes crews make everything possible. They are incredible.

By the weekend of March 28, I was becoming concerned about getting to and from work safely, and how we were going to manage to protect ourselves in the studio. Health care professionals and government officials weren't being clear about who should wear masks. At one point, it was advised that only health care professionals should wear them. It was soon suspected that the reason behind that was to stop a run on masks and save the supply for doctors. Again, this may sound shortsighted and overly concerned about scarcity, but during the early months of the pandemic, that's just the way it was. People were buying up masks online, along with many common household items. Even toilet paper became a scarce resource.

In the studio, the staff was downsized to allow for social distancing. The camera operators started wearing masks. Sometimes I'd get a paper or packet delivered to me by someone unmasked, but it was rare. The main people unmasked were us, the on-air talent. We started covering topics about asymptomatic people spreading the virus without realizing it, and in turn getting someone else very sick. How could we even manage that possibility?

Every day, I took a car service to and from work. The driver was masked, but I didn't know who had been in the car before me. I asked some of the city's top doctors what the likelihood was that the virus could linger in the car and infect me. They didn't know. I would sit in the back seat with my head sticking out the window. When I got home, I'd take my shoes off outside the apartment door, toss all of my clothes in a dry-cleaning bag, and shower before hugging Daddy and you.

I was terrified that I would get you sick. I was overcome by this need to protect you from something none of us understood.

You were four months old when the coronavirus hit its stride in New York City. We were living in Manhattan, a tiny island crowded with almost four million apartment dwellers, commuters, and tourists on any given day, bumping into and breathing all over one another. Translation: a potential hotbed for the transmission of disease.

Our apartment building was quite large, with ten apartments per floor and almost fifty floors. Worse, we were still in a one-bedroom, which we had planned to move out of when you hit the six-month mark. A small kitchen, small living room, a bedroom, and 1.5 baths. Moving wasn't an option at that point because there was no way to visit apartments in person without feeling unsafe, and real estate agents had, for the most part, stopped showing them in person anyway. The prospect of a moving company with multiple people trekking in and out of our apartment also seemed unwise. So we were stuck in that apartment for a while, for better or worse.

I became hyperaware that if one of us got sick in that little space, all of us probably would. I had also just stopped breastfeeding you a week earlier. My very early morning work shift and long block of time in the makeup chair and on-air made it difficult to pump milk, so I started missing two pumping sessions a day. My milk production quickly got all messed up and I had to bring in the best formula I could find. *If I get exposed to COVID, he won't get antibodies*, I kept saying to myself. I felt guilty, like I had already let you down.

In the midst of all this, you went through a sleep regression. You had trouble going down, you were waking up throughout the night, and you were fussy in the morning. It was very hard to get you to sleep, and Daddy and I weren't sleeping much at all. We were all exhausted.

Knowing what I know about the importance of sleep and its relationship to good health, I started to worry. *My body isn't in a good state to be exposed to this virus*, I thought over and over. It had been less than five months since I had delivered a baby, I hadn't slept well since then, and now I wasn't sleeping much at all. I upped my supplements, but the lack of sleep was key and I knew it. There were many times I wondered if I should be calling out from work, but I couldn't do it. I had a job to do. A job I valued. A job I wanted to do. I was part of a team, at work and at home, and I didn't want to let either team down.

It was a confusing, frustrating time. For everyone.

I wanted to do my job, and so I talked myself into it, every weekend. *You're going to be fine,* I told myself, while wiping down everything I touched or came near. The pediatrician once explained to us that the immune systems of babies are more fragile before six months of age. I couldn't stop thinking about that.

For the March 28 weekend show, I requested to work out of a small pod on another floor. They made that happen for me. It sounded like a good idea at the time, a secluded space removed from others. But while in there, I started thinking: *Wait a minute, was this smart? Who was in this tiny space before me? Did they sneeze in here and now it's all condensed in this small area?* All I could think of every day was your tiny immune system. And the breast milk you no longer had.

It was all crazy-making.

On Sunday, March 29, after we wrapped the morning's live show, I went home. Sitting in the back of the car, I felt exhausted. I wasn't sleeping, was trying to do my job, didn't want to disappoint anyone. The exhaustion I was feeling made sense.

I did a little checklist in my mind:

Nutrition? *Yes. I'm eating well.*

Supplements? *Of course. Taking them all.*

Exercise? *Always.*

Sleep? *Um, what's that again?*

Stress? *Oh. Well. Hmm.*

I stopped thinking about it.

The car made its way across town to our Upper East Side apartment, the window beside me wide open. I pulled out my phone and looked at photos of you. Smiling. Laughing. Seriously intent, holding my finger. Sleeping in Daddy's arms. Pictures of you always make me happy. They get my endorphins going. But this time, the images sparked a fear in me.

I put the phone down and took in the sky. There were so many clouds that day. I got home to our apartment and dove into my time with Daddy and you. The feeling of exhaustion remained, but I tried to push it aside, recharged in the love of our trio.

A day or so later, I started to get weird headaches. I don't generally get headaches unless I'm sick, and I hadn't been sick in so long. I couldn't recall the last time I had the flu or a cold. Yet there I was, suddenly getting headaches. I figured I had reached my sleep-deprivation limit. I also started sweating a lot, almost like waves of profuse sweating. I called the doctor and she reminded me that I had just stopped breastfeeding and my hormones were likely going wild. Sweating was an expected side effect. I listened, but I knew my body. Something wasn't right.

A day or so later, I started feeling a little sick. I took my temperature. It was 99.5. I called Grandma.

"Mom, I have COVID."

"No. No, you don't."

"I do, Mom. I know my body. I've got it."

Grandma couldn't handle that possibility, so she refused to consider it.

When I went to bed that night, I looked around the room. Daddy next to me, you in your crib, all of us in our cozy circle of slumber in the bedroom. *I can't have this virus*, I kept thinking. *How in the heck will I quarantine in eight hundred square feet?* I considered the layout of our apartment. The bedroom, with its full bathroom, the small living room with its East River view and half bathroom, a kitchen so small we often joked that our juicer, blender, and food processor were at each other's throats. The closet? Could someone fit in there, squished up tight? No. I knew the landscape. *This cannot happen.* And if it did, we were all going to get sick because there was no quarantining to be had.

As I lay awake in bed that night, I thought about how before you were born, a family friend had told me I should "buy a box of masks ahead of time because you never know what will happen." She had gotten a terrible flu when her baby was just three weeks old, and those masks proved vital. I had a big box of N95 masks on hand in the closet and had started wearing a mask on car trips to and from work even when I had the window wide open.

By 10:00 p.m., I had a fever of 101. Daddy and I moved you from the crib to the living room bassinet, which we had almost gotten rid of a week earlier because you were just about too big for it. Daddy shifted to the couch.

I knew that I needed to get a COVID test.

But I also already knew that I had it.

I woke up the next morning and felt sick. I had the same fever, with some chills. I was able to get ahold of a doctor friend who said that her friend was testing people. She said he would step outside his office and swab me. This was a big deal, as COVID tests were very hard to come by back then and doctors weren't seeing patients with COVID-related symptoms in person. I put on an N95 mask, wrapped a scarf around the lower half of my face for extra protection, and avoided all interactions outside my apartment. I kept my distance from everyone, entering my building elevator alone and sanitizing the button before and after I touched it. I then made my way to his office. The city was remarkably empty. I saw a handful of people during my walk, but we were very spread apart. When I arrived outside, I texted the number my friend had given me, and the doctor came out with a test kit in hand. I bent my head back, got the swab, the deep one that went all the way back, back, back—whoa.

That night, I had a fever of 102. I quarantined myself in the bedroom and started wearing an N95 mask whenever I left the room. I'm a big germaphobe anyway, so I only needed to up my game of cleaning, sanitizing, mopping, you name it.

Then the test came back confirming what I knew. I had COVID.

I was nervous. I didn't know what would happen to my body because none of the doctors I trusted could tell me what would happen. I knew I hadn't been sleeping, that my body was still healing from childbirth, breastfeeding, and hormonal ups and downs. I had Lyme disease several years ago and knew that it affected my neurological system at the time. I worried that COVID might bring back those symptoms.

Hartley, all of the worst thoughts ran through my mind. What if I got really sick and hospitalized and couldn't see you? What if Daddy got sick, too, and neither of us could take care of you? Where would you go? What if something terrible happened to us or to you? I couldn't bear any of those thoughts, but I also couldn't stop thinking them. I hated where my mind was going.

I went to bed with a fever and woke up with a sore throat. Then I'd nap with the sore throat and wake up to heaviness on my chest. Every twelve hours, I felt like I was in a different body. I had a little oximeter delivered from the pharmacy, a tiny device you put on your right pointer finger that measures your oxygen. Mine was consistently at 99 percent, but my lungs didn't feel right. I was an athlete my whole life and could tell that my breathing was compromised. I was texting two top doctors for help, and both of them held the line of 2020: "I don't know."

They advised me to keep checking my oxygen and to let them know if it dropped.

My mind kept going to the darkest places.

The next morning, the third day of my COVID symptoms, something changed inside me. And you're the reason why. I woke up, went into the living room, and looked at your little face. You looked up at me, touched my mask, and smiled the biggest, most beautiful smile you had ever made.

My whole heart lit up.

Okay, Bila, you knocked out Lyme disease. You can do this.

I walked into the kitchen with resolve. I upped my supplements and phoned the holistic center that had helped me overcome Lyme disease. They shipped out some additional supplements immediately. I rinsed my mouth and gargled with sea salt and warm water constantly. I kept my lungs moist by boiling a pot of hot water, then placing my head over the pot, a towel over my head, and breathing in the warm air several times a day. I was missing my celery juice and couldn't get a delivery, as they were all backed up. So I juiced every other vegetable and fruit in the house for the next few days.

Then, one night, Daddy woke up and said: "It's really hot in here. I feel like I'm sweating."

Me: "Oh my God, you have a fever. Take your temperature now."

We did. It was 101. I started crying.

Your daddy shrugged in that stress-free way he shrugs in times of crisis. "I guess I probably have COVID?"

As you know, Daddy has the unique gift of never worrying about anything, ever. The ceiling could cave in and he'd ask me if I was hungry. I pray every day that you inherit that gift.

My heart was racing. I hated myself for having gotten him sick. I looked at him with tears in my eyes, completely apologetic, and he looked back at me, smiled, and asked if I wanted something to eat. I didn't. Who could eat at a time like that? Your daddy. Off he went, walking around the apartment eating ice pops, while I spiraled into an Oscar-worthy performance of what-will-happen-to-us-if-the-worst-possible-scenario-happens-to-us?

I was total insanity juxtaposed to his total calm.

Daddy: "Worry isn't gonna help."

Me: "You know nothing about anxiety if you think saying that to a person with anxiety will help a person with anxiety!"

I panicked some more. "You have to wear a mask around the baby."

He did. Of course.

But then I called the pediatrician for advice on how to protect you, and she said: "It's very likely the baby has already been exposed."

My stomach sank. I, the person who protected you in my belly for nine months, had brought a deadly virus home to your little body.

I was heartbroken. I cried a lot, worried that the only people you had in the world at that moment were two sick people, two people who could get *you* sick. The fear remained with me for a while. I knew the source, but I couldn't control it. We were also stuck in that tiny apartment, with no access to the outdoors or sunshine, and I'm sure that wasn't helping.

"What will happen to him, Jeremy?" I would cry beseechingly to your daddy. "My parents can't come get him. I won't let them. What if he has it and gives it to them?"

Then, the worst of my worst nightmares came true. COVID hit you.

It began when a tiny patch of eczema you'd already had exploded into full-blown body eczema. Your back, arms, legs, and torso were all covered in patches of rough, dry, itchy, scabbing skin. Even your little feet. Your hiney and face cheeks flared up. I couldn't get you in to see any doctors, so Daddy and I held your little body up to a camera for multiple doctors to examine you virtually. The medical consensus was that exposure to COVID had revved up your immune system, and the eczema was your body's heightened immune response. We were told scratching would only make it worse. I felt so bad for you. I couldn't imagine my whole body itching like that.

I researched organic, plant-based lotions, and tried more than I can remember, but I knew that this would have to run its course through your little body. We even tried some prescription creams I wasn't crazy about using, but they didn't help much. We put little mittens on your hands, little socks actually, to prevent you from scratching. You'd try to bite them off and would sometimes succeed. The itching was relentless and I hated seeing you uncomfortable. We bathed you in warm water (thank you for loving bath time so much) with special botanical ingredients, then rushed you onto the changing table so we could lotion your slippery body while it was still damp. You, of course, thought this was hysterical and would laugh at us as we tried to complete the process in record time, like it was an Olympic event.

Nothing we did seemed to help the itch. Luckily, that was your only COVID symptom, at least the only one we detected.

And what did you do during all this? When you weren't wiggling your body around from the itch, you continued to laugh, snuggle, and smile. We tried everything we could to relieve your discomfort, and we must have looked downright silly to you, because you'd return our efforts with a chuckle and the sweetest twinkle in your eye. You were so resilient, so inspiring.

Of course, our dog Daisy was unaffected by everything, running around like a maniac as usual the entire time. She'd sprint from one end of the apartment to the other, and you'd laugh like crazy. Perhaps she was your inspiration, like you were ours.

Daddy and I were committed to finding ways to laugh during those difficult weeks. I swear, if anyone had put a camera in our apartment and filmed, I'm pretty sure I'd have a comedy series by now. Daddy pacing mindlessly about, eating ice pop after ice pop, me delivering dramatic monologues morning and night, the dog bouncing off the walls. And you, well, enjoying life like nothing was happening. Minus the itch, of course. You even got an enormous kick out of our masks when we first had them on. You'd pull on them and smack them and get yourself into a fit of laughter.

My symptoms mostly lifted after about a week and a half, Daddy's a little sooner. I started to exercise, focusing on less rigorous activities like yoga and stretching. For about a month, I would get this odd sense of temperature deregulation that would come and go. I'd almost feel like I was coming down with something, and then it would just lift away. My lungs weren't 100 percent for several months either. I was fine walking around and was able to exercise, but having been a runner and an athlete, I could tell that things weren't as they should be. My tests would come back normal, but I knew my body. It wasn't quite healed yet, but would be soon.

Two (long) months after your eczema explosion, it worked its way out of your body, for the most part.

I felt so many emotions as we emerged from that stressful time. More than anything, I felt incredibly lucky. Lucky to be alive, lucky to have come out of it all with our health intact, lucky to have this incredible baby who smiled and laughed the whole time, and kept us smiling and laughing too. Your perfect little contagious giggle boosted all of our immune systems.

You were our hero. And still are.

When you get scared in life, Hartley, remember to believe in yourself. Believe in your strength. Believe in your family and friends to support you, and in your ability to do the same for them. Look for the good things in even the bleakest of moments. Empower your body's recuperative forces in every way you can.

I bought you that "Be Brave" T-shirt because you were so brave.

You did it. And you could do it all again if you had to, with just as many smiles and just as much laughter.

Challenge the fear, Hartley. Give it a run for its money. And when you do, think of your sometimes too-dramatic mama, who believes in you every step of the way.

I love you more than life,
Mama

Mealtime

Dear Hartley,

Mealtime. It's so simple, yet so complex. Deciding what to eat, cooking all of the ingredients, getting the table set and drinks poured, gathering the household members in one space at one time to enjoy a meal. It's not always easy, but it's always worth it.

When your daddy and I first started feeding you, we made many mistakes. First-time parents do all kinds of silly things. For starters, your mama spoon-fed you for way too long. I had started out right, placing purees on your tray and inviting you to explore them on your own. But I got nervous when I felt like you weren't eating enough, micromanaged the situation, and decided that I knew better than you did how to get you fed. I was wrong.

Luckily, we figured out how to backtrack our mistake and get you in the self-feeding zone.

I also made another big boo-boo. I was so focused on you ingesting enough food, on your meal being perfectly balanced, that I got into the bad habit of feeding you separately from us—first, actually—and then Daddy and I would eat lunch while you napped and dinner when you went to sleep. It felt completely odd, but with the two of us working from home and so many chores to do in a day, it enabled us to focus on one task at a time. Get you fed first, and the rest would follow.

That way of doing things also enabled me to obsess about what you were and weren't eating, another mistake. I had been trying to make the whole feeding situation less stressful by feeding you separately, and had instead made it more so. I also didn't take the time to realize that you would be missing out on eating *with* us, on a family dinner experience that would be important to your development. I was stuck in my head yet again, but was soon to get out of it.

I remember the first time we changed course and sat down together to eat, all three of us, at the same time. You were so much more relaxed. You scooped what you wanted off your tray into your mouth with your little fingers and smiled. You'd watch Daddy and me talk, and pay attention to our gestures. I could see that you were learning. Even if you weren't manifesting those skills yet, you were absorbing so much. You even picked up your little spoon and put it in your mouth, which you had never, ever done before. Most importantly, the whole experience was much lighter and happier. I had finally taken the pressure off, and everyone felt better. You liked being at the table with Mama and Daddy, and I kept thinking, *Of course he does. How foolish was I not to realize that this is the most important part?* Sometimes when you have a child, you're so focused on doing what you *think* is best for them, that you forget to pause and consider you might be wrong.

Life in 2021 feels so busy, Hartley. Technology has made people's lives busier than ever before. Constantly buzzing cell phones, a zillion movies and TV shows on Netflix, Hulu, or Amazon Prime just waiting to be watched with the click of a button, work emails that come in straight through the night, iPads with beckoning games for even the tiniest of tiny tots. Constant distractions are the new normal. Because of that, it's hard for people to wrap their heads around putting it all aside temporarily to just eat dinner. It's not a one-task-at-a-time kind of moment in society right now. People start thinking, *But if I just work while I eat, I'll get twice as much done.* Or, *If I answer these emails during dinner, there will be one less thing to do later.* With emails and texts building up as the day goes on, it's hard to blame anyone for thinking like that.

But in multitasking through meals, we're losing something important as a society.

The dining room or kitchen table is where amazing conversations are born, live, and grow. The dinner table in my house growing up was where we talked about our day, shared our dreams, and even dug into some controversial topics that we often felt differently about.

Mealtime conversations stretch people's minds.

Meals without outside distraction also give us a much-needed break from planning, organizing, or completing assignments. They become a time to just *be*, a chance to laugh, listen, and nourish our bodies. They're an opportunity to connect with the people we love and leave the chores and stressors of the world behind, even for a short time.

Mommy and Daddy don't allow gadgets near the kitchen table, let alone on them. We didn't have to say that rule aloud, it's just how we live. We don't watch TV while we eat or have the radio on. We are present and engaged with each other.

Many people and families around the world lack quality food and proper nutrition. They would give anything to have access to healthy food and water, to be able to sit down at a dinner table and share in an abundance of goods. Some around the world lack companionship and have no one with whom to enjoy a good meal. In our home, we are privileged and blessed to have both food and family, and we should never take those gifts for granted.

So much good can happen at a simple meal.

The feeling of being face-to-face or side-by-side with others while eating something delicious is unique. It puts a special energy out into the world, one of joy and satisfaction. It brings people together too. We all get hungry and we all love eating food we enjoy. Food brings us together in a way that nothing else really does.

Family traditions are also born at dinner tables. In some families, people go around the table expressing what they're thankful for. In others, family members hold hands in prayer. Some families will share a piece of their day one by one. These traditions grow and are passed down to future generations. When you take part in those traditions as an adult, you often remember sharing them with your parents and grandparents as a kid, and that is so warming to your heart.

Whether it's just the three of us at mealtime, with Daisy nearby eating a homemade plate of her own, or if mealtime includes our extended family with Grandma, Grandpa, and other relatives and friends, it always feels wonderful to share a meal together.

I love mealtime with you. I love seeing you smile as you eat your favorite foods. I love hearing you laugh as I eat mine. I hope you'll always love our mealtime together as much as you do today, even when Mama burns dinner and we all wish Grandma had cooked.

I love you more than life,
Mama

Bigger Than You

Dear Hartley,

Organized religion has always been tricky for me. And it's okay if it's tricky for you too.

I spent first grade through my senior year of high school in Catholic school. I liked a lot of what I heard about God, a greater power, believing in the unbelievable, and the whole concept of faith in something much bigger than I am. But I had trouble believing in the idea of regular people as servants of God. That was because some of the people I encountered in those positions didn't behave so well to me or to others. Don't get me wrong, some of the nuns and priests at my school and local church were wonderful and kind and made me feel like I could really talk to them. But others were not so kind, and I was terrified to make a mistake in front of them or speak up about anything around them. I also discovered that some of them didn't practice what they preached, and that bothered me. What I concluded was that for me, nuns and priests felt like regular people, with character flaws just like us. I couldn't get to a place where it made sense to me to confess my sins to a priest or to believe that something had been blessed by one. I felt like I needed God for that. I loved beautiful churches, stained glass, and had such an appreciation for the architecture and history that lived inside those walls. But Mass never spoke to me the way it did to others. I just couldn't find God there.

Now, that doesn't mean I didn't find God at all. I found God in my room at night when I was sad and needed to talk to someone. Or when I was at school and something happened that made me afraid. Or when I achieved something wonderful and felt incredibly grateful. I talked to God in those moments, in my own words, knowing full well that I had no idea what He or She really was. There was something big and strong out there that I felt close to in those moments, something much bigger and stronger than I've ever been.

That's not to say that you will have the same experience as I have. Maybe you will love organized religion and find God in traditional prayers and traditional religious settings. Maybe you will struggle to find God at all.

I hope you do find God, though. I can't really explain it, Hartley, but believing in something much bigger than yourself does something to us humans. It keeps us humble, helps us feel less alone on the loneliest of days, and gives us hope in hopeless times, hope that we'd struggle to manifest on our own. As you grow up, your daddy and I will talk with you about spirituality and religion. We will share our experiences, insights, and feelings. I grew up Catholic and Daddy grew up Jewish. But it will be up to you to figure out what you believe in, what you want for yourself in that spiritual world, and how you want your spirituality to look, feel, and be.

I never connected with official prayers passed down in school. I just couldn't find my feelings in those words. So I made prayer my own. Every night, I say thank you to God and to the universe. It goes something like this:

Thank you for this life and this partner. Thank you for this child and this puppy dog. Thank you for this roof over our heads that I sometimes complain about. Thank you for our health and our sunshine and the health of those we love. Thank you for sticking by me in the moments when I'm not the best version of myself.

Sometimes the thank-yous change a little, but the idea is the same. I believe there's a force out there walking through life with me who I can talk to when I need it most.

I'm not an expert on faith. (Is anyone really?) So I trust my gut and follow what it tells me. In addition to God, I believe in a powerful universe around us, with energy forces we attract and repel. I believe that the universe thrives on goodness. Sometimes what you put out into the universe gets boomeranged right back at you, especially if it's something ugly that the sun and the skies reject. And we all have those ugly days when we toss anger and frustration out there. I believe in angels, too, guardian angels we've known in life that keep an eye on us from beyond.

I always feel like my Poppy, your Great-Grandpa Silvio, is around me when I'm cooking. He was such an amazing cook and my cooking leaves a lot to be desired, as you've learned by now. I'll wreck dinner and say: "Oh, Silvio, don't hate." Of course, I don't know if he's actually near me and can hear me, but it's just a feeling I have. I often feel like my cat Bronte is around us too. Bronte was a big part of my life when I first lived in the city, before I met your daddy. She was my best friend and my favorite movie-watching companion. I have a picture of Bronte on a wall that leads to your bedroom. You point up at it and smile, and you love to touch it and babble to it. You even lean in to give it kisses. I wonder if Bronte is around you sometimes, meowing and keeping watch by your crib. Or, knowing Bronte, stealing the food you drop on the floor by your high chair.

During the COVID pandemic, I was heartsick for the people who passed away and their families. I was worried for those who lost jobs and businesses they had worked their whole lives to build. I talked to God and the universe about it all, hoping they could send strength to everyone who needed it. I also became deeply appreciative of the gift of life, the little things like waking up to sunshine and soaking some of it up with you before breakfast. I'd thank God, the universe, nature, the beautiful trees around us, the animals, the sky, and the sun that gives us the vitamin D we need so much. I'd look forward to putting my feet in the ocean and the sand again one day.

Think of these big forces of nature like food, Hartley. They feed our souls so much.

My hope is that you will know the feeling of believing in a force much bigger than yourself, that you can confide in that force in times of need, and that you have the courage to discover how you really feel about God, religion, prayer, and the sky above. Don't be afraid to make prayer your own, to let go of the idea of what someone told you it should be and instead discover what it is for you. Don't be afraid to ask questions and talk through doubts. Doubts, much like fear, are an important part of being a real human with real feelings and a real journey.

When in doubt, look up at the sky, take a deep breath, and just start talking. You may be surprised by what or whom you discover.

I love you more than life,
Mama

Labels Are for Packages (and You Are Not a Package)

Dear Hartley,

Nuance. It has become a bad word somehow.

Gray areas. No one talks about them much.

But we should. And I will.

Democrat, Republican, liberal, conservative, vegan, vegetarian. These labels, and so many others, mean very little in the way of telling anyone what you actually value and the kind of life you're actually living. Wouldn't it be easier to just toss the labels and instead share the things you hope for and love, the foods you eat, and the values you hold dear?

Sometimes the same label can even mean completely different things to different people. To one person, "vegetarian" means not eating meat and living on cookies and cake. To another, it means a diet of whole, plant-based, nutritious foods. To one person, "liberal" aligns with high taxes and government overreach. To another, it correlates with education funding and preserving the environment. To one person, "conservative" is synonymous with debt reduction and limited government. To another, it represents religious zealotry and a disdain for multiculturalism.

Labels are inherently, dare I say, dumb. They are a way to box us into some pre-packaged image that rarely fits who we are as whole people.

I didn't always feel this way and used to utilize labels myself. I even titled my first book *Outnumbered: Chronicles of a Manhattan Conservative*. And then I realized I was more of a libertarian...except for this issue here and that one there. Finally, I just realized I was a thinking person and didn't want to be boxed in at all. Thinking human. I guess that's my "label."

Heck, I might even grow a bit (say what?) and change my mind (say it ain't so!) on some issues over the course of my life. A sacrilege, I know.

Labeling others is just as silly and unproductive as labeling ourselves. Deciding you know who someone is and what they stand for based on a label, before they even open their mouth, stops a conversation before it starts.

Labels feed preconceived perceptions of people that are often wrong.

I don't play the label game. And most people out there in the world don't see themselves as fitting into absurd boxes. Unfortunately, many with big microphones make them think that they should fit into those boxes. That helps the people with big microphones gain more power and more money by portraying the world as us vs. them, where they're your ally and the other guy or gal, with some other dumb label, is your enemy. Then they tell you that you must listen to them and trust them, with their big microphone in hand, because it's your only path to the truth.

Hogwash.

Your path to the truth is through yourself, not through some person with a big microphone.

There are industries that thrive on these ridiculous labels. And if you find yourself in one of them, I invite you to be different.

Just be a person.

With thoughts.

That's all. Stand out by simply saying what you think. Real people out there relate to that because they, too, are thinking through things just like you. In the game of life, the best ticket to understanding yourself and others, and forming quality relationships with all kinds of people with all kinds of views, is to just see people as people.

I've had jobs where I've watched people dig in their heels so hard defending a politician or talking point that the next thing you know, they are falling over backward to maintain that position long after it makes sense to anyone, themselves included. If that sounds silly, it's because it is.

It's much, much easier to just be your honest self in every given moment.

If you change your mind on something, say it.

If you feel you were wrong on something, admit it.

Flexibility of thought is a beautiful thing.

I hope your generation is the one that says what I wish I'd said right from the start of my career:

I'm going to be me.

I'm not going to pigeonhole myself for anyone.

I have a brain and I want to use it.

I change my mind and I'm okay with that.

I leave plenty of room to be persuaded.

I want a real conversation and won't settle for less.

Never stop being you. No boxes or labels needed.

And always say what you really believe, knowing full well that someone just may change your mind.

I love you more than life,
Mama

Hulk Baby

Dear Hartley,

Squats were always the worst. But there I was, in the gym, in the middle of a set. A trainer I had bought some sessions with was watching closely. "Let's go," he said. What else could I do? I had no choice, I had to do them. Deep breath in, shoulders back, here we go. Breathe in, and down, down, down, almost to the floor. Exhale, and up, up, up. Look into the mirror to check on your form, and...

Wait a minute.

Who? Is? *That?*

Some guy behind me was jumping from the floor all the way up to foam mats piled super high on top of one another. He was landing without falling too. How was he doing that? Did he have springs in his feet?

I finished my workout. I went to dry off with a towel and grab some water. Next thing I knew, my trainer and Mr. Jumps So High were standing right next to me.

"Jedediah, this is Jeremy. Jeremy, Jedediah."

I acted nonchalant. But really...how was he jumping like that? I had to know.

As it turns out, that jumper and I have been working out together ever since.

That man, of course, was your daddy.

Exercise is very important to Daddy and me. It keeps us sane, smiling, and sleeping well at night. It also keeps us vibrant enough to chase after you, our little ball of endless energy.

I started exercising in high school. My high school was pretty academically intense and I needed something to balance it out, to release my stress and recharge.

But exercise didn't become part of my life until I almost went down a bad path for my body and mind first...

In my sophomore year of high school, I met someone at a hair salon who asked me if I was interested in hair modeling. I had never thought about that before, mostly because my hair was one of the things about myself that drove me nuts. I craved stick-straight hair and mine was, well, not. For a few weeks, I thought about what the person at the salon had said about modeling and figured that maybe I could save some money for college that way. Your grandma and grandpa were on board if it was something I wanted to try. I had some pictures taken by a photographer Grandma found, and I would go into the city now and then to try out for these little modeling jobs. Sometimes I'd even get them. The jobs were interesting, sometimes fun. I met mostly nice people, and I put away some cash.

At one point, I submitted a photo for a model search. I heard back a short time after that I had made the first cut. Grandma and Grandpa drove me out to New Jersey to meet with the agents who would be attending. After we arrived, there was some time for me to get dressed and get myself together, and then I had to walk this little runway before rows of agents. Behind them were parents and guardians. I was too short for runway modeling at five foot four, but I was told the agents were looking for all kinds of girls. I did my little walk, then sat back down with your grandparents and waited.

One of the modeling agents in attendance came over and told us that she was interested in me, but there was a catch. She said that I might have to lose some weight.

I weighed 103 pounds. I was fifteen years old.

She told Grandma outright that I was a little curvy in the rear. Grandma nearly lost it.

So we went home that day without the prize. I hadn't won it by a long shot. Grandma and Grandpa treated me to pizza on the way home. I was okay with not winning the contest, but for the first time in my life, I wasn't enjoying my pizza.

Something bad had happened.

The agent's comment about my weight had gotten in my head.

Then, a perfect storm...

As the demands of my schoolwork became increasingly stressful, I got this idea that I needed something in my life that I could control. Losing weight seemed like the perfect activity. I started cutting out real foods and substituting low-fat garbage. I ate boatloads of pretzels with mustard and fat-free cupcakes. I lied to Grandma and Grandpa about what I was (and wasn't) eating at school. I tossed lunches in the garbage pail and skipped breakfasts altogether.

This went on for a few months. I got down to ninety-five pounds. Grandma was devastated and made an appointment with my doctor and a nutritionist. That week, before my appointment, I looked in the mirror and was horrified. I looked exhausted and withdrawn. I looked sick. I decided that I was done with that unhealthy journey.

I walked right downstairs, fried two eggs, toasted a slice of bread, and ate it all.

I kept the appointment with the nutritionist and listened well. She felt that I had actually shrunk my organs a bit (WHAT?) and that I'd need to rebuild from the inside out. I took her advice and ate a lot of healthy food in the next few weeks.

It felt good. Proper nourishment felt really, really good.

I still felt like I was drowning in academic work, though. It was too often overwhelming. I felt like I had no control over so much of my life, because so much of my life was schoolwork. I wanted an outlet, but I wanted it to be a healthy, uplifting one. I wanted to feel good about my body, and allow my body to help my mind.

I wanted to get into exercise.

I joined the track team and started running long distance. I wasn't competitive about it or focused on the races or the meets. I just really enjoyed the running. It made me feel calm and happy. It cleared my head after hours of homework. Soon enough, I gained my weight back and looked healthy again. I also started to feel strong, and I loved that. Tired muscles helped me to sleep better. When academics felt out of control, I could step outside and go for a run with some of my favorite music in my ears. It was incredibly healing. Even when it was cold out, I would bundle up and get out there. I also learned the power of physical rest, of taking days off from exercise to give my body some room to recuperate. Those days felt good too.

In college, I kept running and added weight lifting and some different cardio options to the mix. I took to the StairMaster pretty quickly.

I've exercised my whole life since then, Hartley, and it has made such a difference in my mental well-being. I even exercised all the way through my pregnancy with you. I sprang for a prenatal trainer a couple of days a week in the second and third trimesters because I wanted to be careful to avoid anything that could harm you, while still giving my body the movement it desperately needed. The trainer also told me something about how "women who exercise when they're pregnant have strong babies." I don't know if that's scientifically true, but it was for us. I definitely had a strong little boy.

When you were delivered, they placed you on your tummy, on top of me, and you held your head up on your own for a really long time. The nurses were stunned. In your first few months of life, you would hold on to toys with such force that Daddy and I would struggle to pry them away. And your kicks were big, powerful kicks for such a tiny person.

One of your favorite activities now is squatting down and picking up anything heavy, like a giant bag of rolled oats. You pick up photo albums and heavy books, leaving us shocked. *How is he carrying those?* One day, while Mommy was getting ready for a spin workout, you grabbed two of my smaller bicycle weights off the floor, one in each hand, and started walking toward me. You then squatted and placed them on the ground. *Weighted baby squats?* Daddy and I were staring at you, mouths open.

You're our little Hulk baby.

We make sure you get the exercise you want and need. Plenty of playground time and lots of physical activity around the house and in our small backyard. You and Daisy are pretty much in constant motion together all day long, playing all kinds of games. You're also up and down the stairs a lot. You seem happiest when you're moving, just like me and Daddy.

Exercise looks a bit different for me these days in that I don't always have a big block of time like I used to. If you need me, that comes first. Even so, several days a week, I make time during your nap or after you go to sleep at night to grab my weights and a mat and get my body moving. Sometimes I'll get a half hour in, sometimes a full hour. Some days, I'll take some time for a short stretching session and a quick meditation to clear my mind and help my body release some of the tension I tend to build up. Other days, I'll just put on some headphones and dance for a little while. Still other days, I rest. Rest is so essential for those muscles of ours.

Exercise doesn't have to fit some standardized fitness definition. It just has to make your body and mind feel good.

The most time I ever went without exercise in my life was six weeks. That was right after I had you. Even when I had Lyme disease and COVID, I took only short breaks, then came right back to fitness to find my center.

For the most part, sweat is my sanity. Boxing, spinning, and weights are my favorite, but I've also come to see the benefits of yoga and getting in touch with my body without so much speed.

Sweat is also my clarity. It helps my creative ideas flow.

When I'm down, exercise lifts me up. When I'm sad, it boosts my endorphins. When I'm confused, it helps me find direction. When I'm nervous, it brings me calm. It's a pretty powerful thing overall.

The great thing about exercise is that it teaches you how to communicate with your body. So when you've done enough and need a little break, it tells you. I always take that break.

You already listen to your body pretty well. You go to the garage door and start babbling at us when you need to get outside. It makes me laugh when you suddenly hop up from whatever you're doing, walk over to the door, start pounding it with your little hand, and give me the "Let's go" look. When we come home from whatever fun outdoor activity we've done together, everything is better. You're calm and happy, we're all happy, it's all for the better. Even Daisy passes out into a good nap after a good walk.

I hope exercise is always something that will help you find your peace. I hope you always care about the deep connection between your mind and your body. You get only one body in this life, Hartley. Help it out and it will help you in return.

My high school track coach used to say, "A strong mind yields a strong body." I think that's true, but it's also "A strong body yields a strong mind." They feed each other well if we allow them to.

We spend so much of our days filled with, and surrounded by, a jumble of thoughts, emotions, responsibilities, toxins, and worries. This all needs to be released. Exercise can help you take out the garbage that builds up in your body, in your mind, in your life.

When in doubt, work it out.

Just start moving.

I love you more than life,

Mama

Trophies

Dear Hartley,

When I was in sixth grade, I really wanted to be on the cheerleading squad. A lot of my friends were trying out and it sounded cool to be able to cheer through our school's basketball games. If I made the team, I'd get a uniform, be able to hang out in a special room before the game, and get to do a halftime cheer just like the ones I had seen college cheerleaders do at games I went to with your grandpa. I was excited. But I was also very nervous about the tryout.

I was so nervous that I blew it.

I delivered all the lines, movements, and jumps properly, but something weird happened because of my nerves, and I was oddly disconnected from what I was saying and doing. It was kind of like an out-of-body experience, like I could hear and see what I was doing wrong, yet I couldn't fix it. I wanted to shout *Smile like you mean it!* or *Stop talking like a robot!* into my ear. It was...bad.

I didn't make the squad. Based on that cheer, I shouldn't have. A girl who is now one of my best friends nailed her cheer and made the team. I remember watching her try out and thinking, *Wow, I really blew it*. I was pretty mad at myself that night. Your grandma did her best to make me feel better, but she had been the captain of her high school cheerleading squad, so I felt pretty silly coming home that day after not making the team.

The reality was that I had messed up my tryout. I had choked, and that was on me.

When the seventh-grade tryout sheet came around, I thought about it, but wasn't quite ready to get back out there. When the eighth-grade sign-up sheets were posted, though, I felt ready to take the plunge. This time, I prepared extra hard. I didn't just memorize the words and movements. I put my personality into my practices. I made the cheers my own. I walked into that tryout all-in, super confident, my energy coming through full force.

I made the squad and it felt great. I couldn't wait to tell Grandma the news.

Right around that same time, I was working hard on a science project with Grandma and Grandpa. I tested the pH levels of bodies of water around Staten Island. I was really into figuring out water pollution, and I wanted to get to the bottom of the cleanest and dirtiest local water supplies. I poured my whole heart into the project, gave a great presentation, and got an A, but I didn't make the science fair. *What? Why not?* Only three projects made the fair that year. When I saw those projects, I realized, *Shoot, theirs are better*.

Here's the thing, Hartley: Sometimes you win and sometimes you lose.

Sometimes you lose because you mess up or don't do your best, like what happened to me in sixth grade with the cheerleading tryouts. Other times, you try super hard, do a great job, put your best foot forward, and still don't make the science fair because, despite all of that, someone else's project was better.

You're probably going to try out for some things in life. You may take part in some competitions too. Spelling bees, athletic matches, science fairs, art festivals, music and dance recitals—you could wind up involved in any or all of those things. Sometimes you'll win and that will feel great. You'll get a shiny trophy that you'll be able to hold up proudly and put on a shelf in your room. Sometimes you'll lose and that won't feel great. You won't get a cool trophy, and instead you'll get a polite "Thank you for trying."

At least that's how it should work.

Right now, there's a silly trend of giving everyone a trophy all the time, no matter how they perform. If you win, you get one. The other forty-nine people who didn't win also get one, and theirs are called participation trophies. The idea is to make everyone feel like a winner so that those who lose don't feel bad.

Nope.

That's not real life. And doing that to kids doesn't prepare them for real life.

Feeling bad is part of life. It stinks, but it happens. Navigating your way out of that bad feeling and getting back out there to try again— that's the real lesson kids should be learning.

Hartley, if everyone gets a trophy, then no one really gets one. Then winning means nothing. Which is wrong, because winning means something.

That's not to say that the person who wins is always the best at what they do, or even that their project or performance is always the best one. People win things all the time that others believe are undeserved. But that's also life. Life doesn't always feel fair. And there's a lesson in that too. Because on the days when it feels unfair, you have the power to either let it eat you up inside or to talk it through and get yourself to a better mental space.

Real life isn't filled with trophy guarantees. Sometimes you get fired. Sometimes you don't get promoted and someone else does. Real life has its disappointments, and it's my job to teach you how to handle those days. It's my job to empower you to pick yourself up and find your way back to a place of trying again.

It's not my job to pretend you won when you didn't.

Growing up, there will be wins and losses. You'll also have some almost-wins, which can be the most difficult losses of all.

When I was sixteen, I had an audition for a national advertising campaign. The winner had the chance for a career-making opportunity. Lots of money, lots of recognition, lots of doors waiting to open. Which ended up happening for the girl who won. I, on the other hand, came in third and walked home with nothing. It was a pretty gut-wrenching loss. Coming close is really tough sometimes, and that night was a rough one for me. Grandma and Grandpa were there for me, just as Daddy and I will be there, in times like those, for you.

If you lose a game or an opportunity, I will do everything I can to help you feel better. I'll be right there with a great big hug and an offer to grab some of your favorite food. But I'll also be there to remind you that losing is a real part of life that helps us grow up. It helps us to consider if, and how, we could've done better. It strengthens us. It's important to call a loss what it is, to learn to cope with it, and to find the passion to move onward and upward.

Win or lose, Hartley, trophy or no trophy, I will love you like crazy. I'll be inspired when you try your hardest. I'll understand when your nerves get the best of you. I'll empathize when you just don't put your best foot forward.

And I'll be just as proud when you pick yourself up from a loss as I will be when you win.

I love you more than life,
Mama

Manhattan

Dear Hartley,

You'll come to find that a place—a location—can be an important part of your journey. Where you choose to live will dictate a lot about who you meet and what you get to do.

Manhattan was a big part of my life until the summer after you were born. Throughout my life, I lived in seven apartments in six different Manhattan neighborhoods. It was quite a journey filled with love, hope, some grief and disappointment, and so many laughs.

I moved from Staten Island to Manhattan when I was twenty-one for graduate school. I stayed for a couple of years, then left for a few, and moved back to the city when I was twenty-six. I lived in the city, minus one year in Brooklyn, for another fifteen years. (Ha. It always drove my outside-of-NY friends crazy when I'd call Manhattan "The City," as if there were no other city in the world.)

I guess it felt like the center of my universe for a really long time.

When I think about how many life changes I went through on that little, busy island, it boggles my mind. I went from being a Columbia student, to cocktail waitressing at a Downtown lounge and a Midtown hotel, to teaching at an Upper East Side school, to being part of the wonderful worlds of two very different television networks. There were times when I was broke, in debt, totally lost, and then suddenly got a big break. There were other times when I was riding high, on my way to fulfilling my dreams, only to be knocked out by a curveball.

I experienced the tragedy of the Twin Towers firsthand, running from my office building and landing in a stranger's apartment where she let me use the phone to call my family and friends and tell them I was okay. We wound up sitting on her floor and talking for hours, bonded in a way I could never have imagined with a complete stranger. We shared tears, fears, and so much confusion.

I waited tables at a two-story lounge until 4:00 a.m. in my mid-twenties. Those were tough shifts with way too many stairs, but I learned a lot from that job. I would sometimes get out early at 2:00 a.m. and go dancing at a nearby club that played '90s music. We'd follow that up with snacks at the corner diner, laughing until the sun came up.

I took movement classes at the American Academy of Dramatic Arts that seemed silly to me at first, but got my body connected to my mind in a way that I hadn't been prepared for. It was life-changing.

I also had some ridiculous dates in Manhattan and learned some good lessons. Those dates helped me to recognize what I did and didn't want in my life. They gave me valuable insights into the kind of character traits I wanted in a man. Those dates gave me the perspective that would help me open up to your daddy one day.

One of my favorite things to do in Manhattan when I was stressed or had been through a tough day at work was to put on my headphones and take evening walks. The East Village was usually my go-to spot. It was unbelievably crowded most of the time, but that's why I loved it. Somehow the noise and the crowds brought me incredible peace back then. It used to drive my best friend insane because he would worry about me wandering around alone, but there was something about nighttime roaming in the city that cleared my head like nothing else.

One of the coolest things that happened to me as a result of living in Manhattan all those years is that I now have the best malarkey meter in the world. I can spot nonsense a mile away. Sniffing out earnest hard workers vs. snake oil sellers is a résumé-worthy skill set I've earned, compliments of New York City.

But the very best thing that happened to me in Manhattan was meeting your daddy when we both landed in a gym on Fifty-Fourth Street and Eighth Avenue.

I learned a lot in that city that never sleeps.

I learned how to find complete peace in the midst of total commotion and chaos.

I learned how to get seventy-five things done at once and still have energy and time to spare.

I learned how to make some really tiny apartment spaces feel homey and welcoming.

I learned how to fall in love fully and completely, and I began the journey of sharing a life with someone.

It's a good city.

It's a strong city.

It's a one-of-a-kind city.

And even though it suffered so much during the pandemic, with businesses closing shop and residents moving out, it will be back.

It's a strong city.

It's a one-of-a-kind city.

Manhattan toughened me up for what was ahead. And what's still ahead.

Always take the time to think about the place you live, Hartley. Choose wisely if you can. Really discover it. Breathe it in. Savor the food and explore the hidden streets. Let it teach you and grow you.

And when it's time to go, honor that feeling too.

I love you more than life,
Mama

Room at the Table

Dear Hartley,

It was that quiet time on a late Saturday afternoon when the hum of daytime traffic slows and the buzz of evening activity hasn't yet come alive. The last rays of sunlight were making their way through your great-grandparents' Brooklyn apartment window. Nanny, my grandma, stood in front of the kitchen counter. She was dipping chicken cutlets into an egg mixture, then flipping them around in a seasoned breadcrumb combination, then placing them in a giant preheated frying pan. Poppy, my grandpa, was close by, stirring his secret tomato sauce, pasta at the ready on the back burner. My parents and I were gathered in a small dining area right off the kitchen, as were a few of my aunts and uncles. A sliced loaf of Italian bread, fresh mozzarella, and an antipasto with olives, peppers, and Italian sausage rested on the table, and we had already started digging in. We had come together to talk, laugh, and enjoy that special time. I know that most Italian families do Sunday dinner, but in our house, we often added Saturdays into the mix.

I was only six or seven, but I knew enough to realize that I was happily surrounded by my family, a group of people who were rich in Brooklyn accents and stories that kept us laughing for hours beyond. I knew that I loved them and that they loved me. I also knew that I was lucky to have them all in my life.

Families come in all shapes, sizes, colors, and combinations. They all look different. We have a small family. Some people have large families. There are mixed-race families, single-gender families, single-parent families, grandparent-led families, and many other possibilities. When it comes down to it, what's important is that each person in a family feels respected, loved, and cared for. You will encounter friends in life who have families very different from yours. Any family that offers safety and support can be beautiful, nurturing, and a gift to everyone who gets to be a part of it.

As I sat in that little dining area outside my grandparents' kitchen as a child, there were a lot of things I didn't understand just yet. What I did know was that every one of those people would move mountains for the others, and that helping to make one another smile was something we all did without even thinking. That meant everything to me as a little person beginning to learn about the world.

My family worked well for me when I was growing up. I didn't have a dog to be my best buddy like you do, but I did have a cat named Scungilli that I would play with all the time. I had this little stick with yarn attached to it that I'd drag on the ground. Scungilli would go insane chasing it, and I'd burst into laughter watching him. Nanny had a lot of siblings, twelve sisters to be exact, each one more hilarious than the next. And my parents' close friends became family, too, sharing in holiday celebrations, barbecues, and weekend dinners at Nanny and Poppy's. There were a lot of loving people and plenty of laughter around me as a child.

I'm hopeful that by the time you read this, you will feel that your family, our family, works well for you too. I imagine that what your daddy and I define as family will be an ever-growing, dynamic coming-together of good people who love you dearly—blood family, good friends, caring neighbors.

In our house, Daddy and I espouse a very inclusive parenting style. We make room at our table for those who adore you, love you, and want to encourage you and help make your journey the best one possible. Everyone brings something different to the table, and we feel that those different life experiences and life choices will help grow your mind and excite your senses in positive ways.

When it comes to raising you, Daddy and I wanted nature and outside time to be a big part of your life right from the start. There's so much to learn from how flowers bend gracefully in the wind, how sunshine reflects in bodies of water, and how fresh snow feels beneath your boots. Nature is resilient and inspiring. When we moved to Staten Island during the early days of the COVID pandemic to be closer to Grandma and Grandpa, Grandma felt strongly about getting you outside daily in your stroller. Grandma loves the water, loves living near the water, and wanted you to feel as much of nature as possible around you. She introduced you to the trees and the birds outside, talked to you about the clouds and the sky. There was one tree in particular that you were afraid of because it had funny-looking leaves. Well, not so much funny-looking, but unique. Grandma would walk you by that tree and you'd start to cry and reach for her to pick you up. Daddy got wind of that and started taking you past the tree every day to help you get over your fear. He'd touch the leaves and smile, inviting you to touch them too. Eventually, you did. Now it's your favorite tree, and we can't go past it without you reaching for the leaves.

Grandma says that on your walks together, you have long talks. I'm pretty sure she's doing most of the talking and you're doing most of the listening, but when I ask her what you talk about, she says, "That's between us. Those are our heart-to-hearts." I'm hoping that one of the many gifts you receive from her will be a long-lasting appreciation for talking, listening, and the music of the outdoors.

Even when you were super tiny, you loved books. You'd stare at the covers and try so hard to flip the pages. You quickly got the hang of it. To this day, you'll toss any toy aside for a good book, and we often read together, especially before naps and bedtime. Although we all read to you, Grandpa is your favorite storyteller. As soon as our doorbell rings and Grandpa walks inside, you run over to your toy chest and grab as many books as you can fit in your arms. (As of this writing, that's about seven.) Grandpa does a great job on all the voices—Spot the puppy dog, the little birdies, the farmer, even the buzzing bees. You love tucking into his lap and hearing the world of books come alive. You also love when Grandpa, who happens to be the tallest of our bunch, picks you up and lets you open and close all of the high-reaching cabinets. (Mommy can't even reach those.) He shows you the picture frames in high-reaching parts of our book-cases too. A tiny hand-painted canvas of my first dog, Emma, is your favorite.

Although we couldn't see them much in person during COVID times, your daddy's grandma (your great-grandma) and his Aunt Penina (who lives part-time in Manhattan and part-time in Germany) both got to watch you grow through FaceTime calls and emailed photos this past year. We'd call them while you chased Daisy around in circles in the living room or send videos of you reading, laughing, and hitting the playground for the first time. When you were first born, Aunt Penina even brought you some nontoxic toys back from Germany, the home of many of the organic clothes and toys Daddy and I have purchased for you. She also speaks like seventeen languages. That's a slight exaggeration, but not by much. Maybe you can pick up some new words from her too.

Our dog Daisy, a big part of our family, was your best playmate during COVID quarantine. Because of social distancing, you couldn't really spend time with kids your age. I worried about that a lot, but Daisy really stepped up to the plate and became your buddy. You chased each other around, cuddled, and shared toys. Daddy did this thing where he gets Daisy to chase him in circles, which sent you into the biggest, brightest fit of laughter. You and Daisy even played hide-and-seek, with Daisy finding her way to whichever nook you were hiding in, and you then surrendering in giggles.

Before the lockdown, we had originally planned on having some child care because both Daddy and I work. But once COVID started, we needed a new plan. Daddy and I decided to work together to balance our jobs and caring for you. We also got a lot of help from Grandma and Grandpa, since we were all quarantining close together. It was sometimes tough to juggle it all, a challenge many families felt at the time, but we did our best.

My best friend, Mike, Uncle Mikey to you, decided he was going to help out by cooking some homemade meals and delivering them to us. This worked out well because Uncle Mikey is an amazing cook, the best cook I know, and he thinks healthy living is important, just like we do. You love his food. You love it more than mine, which would be the honest reaction of anyone with taste buds comparing our cooking. Your favorites were his lentil burgers and oatmeal cookies. Last fall, when you turned one, we had a few friends join us outside, and Uncle Mikey made your birthday cake. He even did it Mama-style, with pistachio milk and maple-sweetened icing. You weren't so much a fan of the birthday song or opening presents, but the cake was a big hit.

As you're starting to see, we have different people playing different roles in this diverse family of ours.

Daddy is the calm in the house. As we've established, he panics, well, never. I can remember the first time you fell on the playground. I was there with you by myself because Daddy had gone to the store to get you avocados. You were holding my hand, but you tripped somehow and lunged forward into the slide. You cut your lip on your bottom teeth and it was the first time I saw you bleed. I burst into tears and immediately called Daddy.

"Come back, hurry, he fell and I see blood on his mouth," I said through tears. Daddy rushed back. When he got there, just a few minutes later, you were already trying to get back on the slide.

"He's okay, Mommy, see? He's a big boy. He'll be okay."

Daddy gave me a hug. I was still recovering from my terrified adrenaline rush. When you stumble in the house and it's clear that you're okay but are still crying, Daddy brings you your favorite teddy bear, aptly named Teddy. "Teddy is here. Teddy's gonna make it all better." You smile and pick yourself up.

Daddy was also wonderful at getting you on a schedule, and he has brought order to your life. He has a lot of patience for processes, which I wish I had. He was the one who got your sleep schedule on point. He was focused and committed. He's also the one who got you to first drink from a straw cup all by yourself and pick up little pieces of pancake or avocado toast and feed them to yourself. Daddy is helping you grow up, little by little, all the while standing right beside you so that when you stumble, you know he's right there, ready to remind you that you can do more than you think you can. Once the COVID vaccine came out, there started to be more kids at the playground, and Daddy and I loved watching you learn how to mingle and navigate the swings and slide with kids of all ages.

As for me? I bring all the doting, of course. I was given a lot of affection as a child, so that has streamed right down to you. I kiss you constantly. I have magic kisses for the boo-boos that make them feel better too. I also do a lot in the food department because nutrition is so important to me. It started with breast milk, then we got into homemade fruit and veggie purees, and now we've added organic meats from local farms I've gotten to know and wild fish from a wonderful fish store. I also do a lot of research into nontoxic products like toys, furniture for your room, bath and body products, even clothing. These are my passions, but they became even more important to me when you arrived. There are a lot of wonderful people out there, Hartley, with businesses dedicated to making sure products are free of toxins, pollutants, and all of that icky stuff. My baby shower registry took a long time to build, with lots of focus on ingredients to avoid and others to embrace. I shared it with friends who were hoping to do the same for their little ones.

I also read you a bedtime story every single night, then hold you in my arms for a few minutes and tell you how much we love you, how much God and the angels and the universe love you, and how we're all sending you good vibes for big, beautiful dreams.

Daddy always jokes that I anticipate your every need. Sometimes I do that too much, I'll admit. Daddy is a little better at letting you figure things out on your own. The thing is, you lived inside Mama's body for nine months. Your hunger, thirst, restlessness—they all became my own. Anticipating your needs is kind of like a reflex now. But I know that sometimes Daddy is right, and I need to give you that room to grow.

I'm also the goofball of the bunch. I do silly dances, make weird noises, and do bad cartwheels. I'm here to make sure you don't forget the silliness. It's soul-saving.

And I'm a bit (translation: a lot) more neurotic than Daddy. When you go out to play, I always make sure you have your sweatshirt, sunscreen, a light coat, a hat for the cold, another hat to block the sun if it starts to bother your eyes. I could go on and on. I chase after Daddy and you with more items than I can carry as you head out the door.

I want you to know that your support system will always be here in our family. Even when we disagree, if and when you make decisions that make me go *He did what?*—I'll still be here, right here, with open arms, open ears, and an open heart.

Daddy and I make a good team. We gravitate toward different aspects of caring for you.

I give you a bath, he towels you off and puts you into pajamas. I read your bedtime story and sing you a song, we take turns putting you down to sleep. At the playground, Mama handles the swings while Daddy's a pro on the slide. Of course, sometimes these roles overlap and flip-flop, but the teamwork stays intact. Daddy is a wonderful partner to me, and I love taking care of you with him.

Within our family, we all have different things we do great and not so great. We all have strengths and weaknesses. We all have good days and bad days. No one is perfect. A family will never be perfect because it's made of real, flawed people like you and me. I guarantee you that any family you think looks perfect from afar actually isn't up close. My hope is that our bad days inspire us to do better for one another.

When I was little, my grandpa used to take me out every weekend to the park next to their building. He'd swing me on the swings for what seemed like hours, my feet floating up into the vast blue sky. Your grandma and great-grandma would look out the window and shout, "Don't swing her too high!" Then Poppy and I would go for a slice of pizza and a cherry Italian ice, my favorite.

Nanny watched soap operas pretty often and sparked my interest in acting. She also used to listen to romantic music all the time and gave me a passion for songs and lyrics of the heart. To this day, when I hear "You Light Up My Life," I get misty-eyed thinking of that very tough, rough-around-the-edges Italian lady from Brooklyn who had a soft spot for love songs. I may have inherited a trait or two from her.

Your grandpa was the one who took me to all the great amusement parks like Six Flags Great Adventure in New Jersey, Dorney Park & Wildwater Kingdom in Pennsylvania, and Busch Gardens in Florida. Grandma and Grandpa took me to Disney World together, but it was Grandpa who rode every ride with me, including those spinning ones he didn't like so much. When it came to school, Grandpa taught me a lot about organizing tasks and plowing through challenging projects with discipline. We also talked about practical things like balancing checkbooks and budgeting money, and I've learned to appreciate common sense from him. I'll admit that I'm more impractical, dare I say fanciful, by nature, but the practical part of my brain that Grandpa helped build is such an important balance to the rest of me, and I'm grateful for it.

It was your grandma who got me into romantic movies. She says she watched *The Way We Were* a billion times when she was pregnant with me. That may have something to do with why I was in love with Hubbell Gardiner (a.k.a. Robert Redford) for the first twenty or so years of my life. Grandma is sensitive and empathetic, and she inspired me to feel deeply for myself and others. That inspiration helped me to delve into the emotions of characters I played onstage and on camera. Grandma also treated me to the best of things. She'd save her money so that we could go into Manhattan on special occasions to get hair treatments at this really top-notch salon. She took me on special shopping expeditions for my eighth-grade graduation dress and for school dances and birthday parties. Grandma knew how to put outfits together so that I always looked like a million bucks. She stretched her budget often, cutting back when it came to herself so that she could spend her money on something I'd love. What I loved most, though, was the time we spent together doing those things, enjoying a frozen yogurt during shopping breaks and laughing with our hair wrapped up in all kinds of deep-conditioning concoctions.

I can still see those days vividly in my mind.

When you get older and some of the people in our family aren't here anymore, I hope you will revisit your memories of the time you spent with them and smile with all the tenderness that those people brought into your life. I hope you will remember all of the different people who came to our family table and what they taught you. Those memories, and the lessons you glean from such experiences, will enhance your days and keep you warm and cozy when life gets tough.

One day, you may build a family of your own. You may marry and have children, maybe even grandchildren. Or maybe you'll live in a big old house with a bunch of friends with whom you'll grow old. Or perhaps you'll have lots of cats and dogs, children who purr and bark. There are so many options, who knows what path you'll choose. They can all be wonderful.

As this nation moves toward a place of appreciating the many different combinations of what a healthy, loving family can look like, our country will become stronger, with more powerful bonds between us all.

I look forward to many days of expanding our family table, and to meeting all of the people you'd like to welcome here too.

I love you more than life,
Mama

All Ears

Dear Hartley,

One of the many things I love about you is how you look at Daddy and me with focus when we are sharing something with you. Your eyes get super big and you stare at us intently. As one example, you don't like being on the changing table (okay, you hate it), but once I start telling you a story or Daddy starts singing you a song, you're in. You zero in on our lips and eyes and start smiling with the most amazing focus. Our hearts melt. You love sitting in Grandpa's lap as he reads you your favorite books, and you'll look up at him now and then and smile as he reads. If he inadvertently skips a page or a line, you pull him back quickly to the right spot. When Grandma sings to you, you stop everything you're doing and look into her eyes and listen.

You have this beautiful ability to focus your attention on the person with whom you're engaging, and I hope it's a skill that stays with you your entire life.

I could've learned a lot from you when I got caught up in the start of the tech revolution's gadget frenzy. I was multitasking to the nth degree. I would have a conversation on my phone, with my iPad on my lap, the television on, and my computer nearby. I rarely heard a full conversation. I would hear part of what someone was saying on TV and half of what a friend was asking on the phone, amid a flurry of texts about what my best friend's sister's dog had just eaten off the floor.

It's a wonder I ever knew what was going on around me at all. Maybe I didn't.

Then I had the chance to be on television. I had always loved the television and film industry. I had never thought I'd be talking politics on TV, but it was a good opportunity and I embraced it.

I was thrust into it all pretty quickly. I had been teaching at an Upper East Side private school and writing on a blog when I reviewed a book written by a well-known radio personality. As it turned out, he liked my review and read some of it aloud to millions of listeners on his radio show. Grandpa heard it while driving home from work and nearly lost his marbles. Soon after, a successful television host invited me to be on the panel of his show. From there, I was invited to be on television quite often.

I kept getting called in to do more segments, so I figured I must be doing something right. But something didn't *feel* right.

I just didn't feel like me.

And then one night, after pretaping a segment and watching it air on television hours later, a habit I rarely engage in because it can get super weird to watch yourself on TV, it hit me. I figured out what was wrong.

I had stopped listening.

I had become so focused on what I was going to say next that I had forgotten to listen to what someone else was saying *now*. I had stopped reacting live and sounded like an overprepared, preprogrammed machine. I wasn't in the moment, and that disappointed me because I had always been someone who valued living in the moment. Most of all, I didn't sound like me. I had lost myself in that space somehow. I wasn't a journalist, and didn't want to be one, so I had to remember that. I wasn't a party loyalist either. I was just a gal with opinions, strong opinions, opinions I wanted to share and have challenged.

In addition to losing myself, I had lost my purpose. I was there to have a conversation, a good one. That had been my reason for embracing the whole TV journey to begin with, to have on-air conversations that could make us all think harder, better. And yet, somehow, I had allowed listening, an essential part of any good conversation, to take a back seat.

Prior to being in television news, the only television-like experience I'd had was when I was playing someone else. I had taken classes at the American Academy of Dramatic Arts and performed scenes there. I did a scene study program at Weist-Barron Studios and a film and television showcase in New York and Los Angeles. I even shot some pilots that never made it off the ground. Oddly enough, playing someone else always felt natural to me. But now I was doing this strange thing in TV news where instead of being myself, I was playing some version of myself that I thought the medium, the network, and the audience wanted.

I struggled like this for a bit, making my way only briefly into moments that felt authentic. At some point, I was invited to do a show called *Red Eye*. Its angle was "satirical talk show." It aired at 3:00 a.m. and featured a lot of comedians, as well as eccentric topics that would never see the light of day on a news network, but the stories were good ones. We taped it the evening before it would air, and most of the show was unscripted. The idea was to sit around a table and talk, react, laugh, and live in the moment. The only rule was: Whatever happened, happened. And some pretty funny stuff happened.

I had been hesitant to go on that show at first. I think I was afraid of just being me, worried that there was an expectation that I should be the person I had been presenting on-air by day, even though that person was feeling so disconnected from who I really was. Regardless, I took the plunge and agreed to be a guest. And because it aired in the middle of the night, I felt like I had permission to just be myself. *Maybe no one's watching*, I told myself that first time.

In reality, many were watching. The *Red Eye* fans were some of the most engaged I had ever seen, watching live in the middle of the night and sending hilarious tweets my way that I'd see the next morning. But more than that, my experience on the show brought me back to...me.

I interacted with that group of people in a whole new way.

First of all, I actually interacted.

And reacted.

And participated and engaged and, wait for it—really listened to what they said.

I laughed. A lot. And that felt really good.

To be clear, I'm not a comedian by any stretch of anyone's imagination. But I was in the moment with a lot of naturally funny people, so I occasionally said something utterly ridiculous that the cast would then make funny. I even made the funniest guy on the panel laugh sometimes, which was pretty cool.

I was living in the moment again. As a result, I figured out a way to get my TV energy to match my real-life energy, at least most of the time.

On that show, I even dressed like me. Denim skirts, fun dresses, and logo tees. It felt like a Saturday night out with friends, with some politics and controversial topics thrown in. Soon enough, it would be my favorite show to do on the network. It became the show I did most. Of course, I thought about how that might change my career trajectory, might change the jobs I was offered and the shows I was invited to be on, but it was all okay because this trajectory felt more like me.

I didn't stop doing daytime shows. Instead, I figured out how to be myself there, too, by really listening to what was happening and genuinely reacting. The 3:00 a.m. TV Bila (a.k.a. the real Bila) became the 5:00 p.m. TV Bila and the 9:00 a.m. TV Bila. I was going to be me everywhere, and if people liked what they saw, they'd invite me back. If they didn't, it probably wasn't the right spot for me anyway. I was very much okay with that shift in my world.

One day, I got a call from ABC's *The View*. I had watched the show many times throughout the years and knew that if nothing else, it was a place where good conversation lived. I got the okay to guest-host there while under my Fox contract, and got a job offer from ABC to co-host *The View*'s next season soon after. I knew that the other co-hosts and I would disagree on some things, but it was an amazing chance to have those back-and-forths on-air. I thought that maybe I could help inspire people with different views to have those conversations at home with mutual respect, admiration, and a good ear for listening and living in the moment.

The View was an all-around great time for me. It was a spontaneous kind of show, which I welcomed. Sure, we had morning meetings to choose topics and liked to pick ones that fostered good debate and showcased our different views, but most of what happened on-air was born in the moment. We didn't get into the meat of topics off-camera before a show. "Save it for the show!" Whoopi would say if we started digging into a topic too much in the meeting. She was right. Whoopi knows good TV. Whoopi *is* good TV. She has been doing this for a long time and knows that the best TV moments happen live without fleshing too much out in advance.

I stuck to my mantra: Live in the moment, listen well, and be yourself.

Except one time.

And I've regretted it ever since.

We were talking about a political appointee who was the topic of conversation that week in our country. Merrick Garland, to be exact. I remember the precise moment I got stuck in my head. I noticed that my co-hosts were generally in agreement on the topic and I froze. I stopped listening and got lost in my own thinking. I had been hired to be the "conservative seat" on the show. I felt this sudden, strange obligation to toe a different line from everyone else's.

So I did. I said something that sounded like what I thought the "conservative seat" on the show would say, or should say. As it came out of my mouth, it felt odd, inauthentic, like I was outside my body listening to someone else say what I was actually saying. But it was too late, it was already out there. And for some reason, I was frozen and couldn't take it back.

I regret that moment. People who say they have no regrets in life are usually not telling the truth, Hartley. Everyone has something they regret. That was my regrettable television moment.

No one had encouraged me to say what I said on-air. I had made that mistake all on my own, which was an important acknowledgment because I needed to own my mistake in order to learn from it. I made that misstep because I stopped listening—to the hosts, to my gut, to the conversation we were having. I stopped paying attention to how I actually felt and got caught up in what I thought people wanted and needed me to say.

I never did that again. I vowed to never again stop listening on-air, to never again say something on-air I didn't believe, to never again worry about someone else's possible expectation of who I should be or what I should say. I have kept that promise to myself.

Forget the expectations, Hartley. All of them. Don't spend one second worrying about who people might expect you to be, or what they hope will come out of your mouth. Or what you *think* they hope will come out of your mouth.

Listen to yourself and how you feel.

Hear what the person talking to you is saying.

Listen to the moment unfolding then and there.

I, in turn, vow to always hear what you have to say.

I will try my absolute best to do so without judgment.

I will work hard not to leap to advise before you've really had a chance to say what you're feeling.

And sometimes, I don't have to advise at all. I can just listen.

I love you more than life,
Mama

Character

Dear Hartley,

Character. It's a big word. A big, powerful word.

I remember being in a deli with your grandpa when I was a little girl. We were in line waiting to pay for something when an older gentleman walked into the store and up to the register.

"You accidentally gave me five extra dollars," he said, placing a five-dollar bill on the counter.

"Oh, wow, thank you. That's so nice of you," said the cashier. She smiled and shook her head at her own mistake.

The gentleman smiled back and exited the store.

I saw the cashier breathe a sigh of relief. I didn't realize it then, but if her register had come up short on cash at the end of her workday, she likely would've had to make up the difference out of her own pocket.

I remember asking Grandpa about what I had seen, about why that man had brought the money back.

"That's what we call good character," he said. Or something to that effect. And he continued to explain what that meant. I'm not sure I completely understood his explanation at that very young age, but I gathered that good character had something to do with how you behaved when no one was watching and how you treated people when they had nothing to offer you. It was about doing the right thing, even if you didn't get to keep the five extra dollars someone had given you by mistake.

I remember a TV agent telling me to pay attention to how people treat you when you lose a big job, that it would say a lot about those people's character. That proved remarkably true when I lost a big job a few years ago and watched people who had been adoringly writing me for months suddenly have no use for me. I watched people beg me to come on their television shows so they could get the first few segments with me after I lost that big job. Months later, those same people treated me like I was beneath them, like I wasn't worthy of their time. But I also watched unexpected people treat me with extra kindness back then, knowing that life had tossed me a curveball and that I might need a little extra grace while trying to juggle it.

People reveal their character at all sorts of times, Hartley. But they tend to reveal it most when they have nothing to gain from you. I always see people's character best when I hit a rough spot. Those who stick around and support you in times like those are the ones you want in your life. Those are the people with good character.

Good character shows up in so many ways.

Like when you don't hesitate to admit you were wrong.

Like when you show up in person for tough conversations of the heart.

Like when you do something good when you know that no one can see you, no one will thank you, and no one but you may ever know that you did it.

I can't wait to watch you grow, Hartley. It will be our job—your daddy's and mine, your grandma's and grandpa's—to help you build your character. All of the people who love you will play a role. You should know that the people who treat you badly in life, and there will sadly be some, will also play a role. They will show you how *not* to be, how *not* to treat others or yourself.

You will have a lot of encounters, some fulfilling and fun, some not so fun. You will have highs. You will have lows. You will discover the best and the worst in people. And it will all help to build your character.

Above all else, your daddy and I want you to be kind. Kind to others, to the world, and to yourself. Kind to the planet, to the plants and animals, and to everything we're so lucky to be a part of on this earth.

Pay attention to the people around you with good character. Learn from one another, teach one another, grow with one another.

And when in doubt about what to do in a situation where no one's watching, think of the gentleman who returned that extra five dollars to the deli so many years ago. Think of the smile on the cashier's face. Think of the ripple effect of a small, kind action on the way people feel about themselves and each other.

I love you more than life,
Mama

Romance

Dear Hartley,

Your mama is a romantic.

I also love romantic movies, the kind with strong love stories and rewarding endings, endings that make you feel like the impossible is possible. When I'd talk about those movies with friends in my twenties, I always heard back, "Guys don't really behave like that" or "All of that romance only happens in the movies." Or some version of that.

Life proved them wrong in many ways.

Yes, movies have scripts, often well-written scripts. In the movies, the lead guy will find his words much easier than you ever will, because, yes, they're written for him. In the movies, the weather may turn from rain to sunshine at just the right time, or the timing of a chance encounter may work out a little too perfectly. That's all true. You can't compete with the movies, and you shouldn't try to.

Despite what you'll hear from some friends in your life, no one expects you to be that guy from the movie.

But that doesn't mean you can't do romance well. And in some cases, maybe a little better than it's done in the movies. In real life, good romance is littered with imperfections, and those imperfections can be a lot more interesting than perfectly crafted movie scripts.

Your daddy did a lot of romantic stuff when we started dating, and he still does.

He made me delicious dark-chocolate-almond-butter cups when we first started going out. I had been talking for days about how I wanted to find a good recipe. He found a recipe, made them, and left them in a little box outside my door as a surprise before I headed to work one night.

Daddy surprised me several times with simple getaways outside the city when I was craving the sounds of chirping birds and quiet walks among beautiful trees. Once, he took me to his hometown for an overnight stay, complete with daytime hiking, nighttime cooking, and quiet walks through his childhood stomping grounds. Another time, he surprised me with a cabin getaway that was perfect in its total simplicity. We lit a fire, cooked some food, watched the snow begin to fall, then got out there and had a good, old-fashioned snowball fight. Daddy proposed to me in the small garden of a beautiful bed-and-breakfast, then took me to dinner at an Italian restaurant that looked like it was straight out of Italy, homemade pasta included.

These days, Daddy leaves little Post-it notes around the house with messages that make me smile. One night, he stayed up late making my favorite banana-oat cookies. When I came down for work at 5:00 a.m. the next morning, there was a full plate on the kitchen counter with a "Never skip breakfast" note on top. When he has an errand to run, he'll stop by my favorite health food store and surprise me with my favorite green juice. He says "I love you" a lot too. And I love that about him.

Romance doesn't have to look like some guy in a movie doing everything right. Sometimes romance is filled with adorable mistakes, like the time your daddy planned a picnic right in the middle of an active sprinkler system, which turned on just as we started to eat. We got soaked, but man was that funny.

And yes, of course, I do romantic stuff for your daddy too. I'll surprise him with a food delivery from his favorite restaurant when I know he's had an exhausting day. Daddy also hates to buy stuff for himself like razors, shaving lotion, or any basic things like that. I'll order those products when I see him running low and leave them on the bathroom counter with little "Time for a refill" notes. When I visit my favorite holistic center on Long Island, I stop by one of your daddy's favorite cafés and surprise him with two large lentil soups and a giant chocolate chip cookie. That's his lunch of champions. And sometimes I'll just take a pause with him while you nap, cuddle him up, and tell him how lucky I am to share my life with him. I do a lot of, "Do you know how much I love you?" And I mean it. I love your daddy like crazy.

I don't know what romance will mean to you, Hartley. I don't know how you'll feel about it at all. But for me, romance is really simple. It's about loving someone so much that you want to show them that love. It's about thinking of little, unexpected ways to make them smile. It's about hearing what they need and seeing if there's a way for you to bring some of that into their day.

As you go through life, I know you'll meet people you really care about. If you're lucky, you'll fall in love. Just remember, you don't have to be that guy in the movie. You just have to be you. You don't need a perfect script or a perfect soundtrack to let someone know how special they are to you. Do it your way, from the heart, and I know it will be wonderful.

I love you more than life,
Mama

Friendship

Dear Hartley,

Mama keeps her circle small, as you know, but my friends are really good ones.

I can tell them anything and know that they would never share my secrets.

I can talk about my fears and doubts without worrying they'll dismiss me.

I can bounce creative ideas off of them and know that I'll get great suggestions and advice.

They're honest, funny, genuine people who care about me, Daddy, and you.

Good friends are so important. There is nothing like knowing you can pick up a phone and get the support or laughter you need. There's nothing like knowing you've met people along the way who are invested in your happiness, who advise from a place of goodness, and who you'd trust with your heart, your dog, your child.

I met my first real best friend in the sixth grade. I met my second and third in college. I spoke with all three of them this week, and I speak to two of them very often. Sometimes it takes time to meet the people who will stick with you through life, the ones you *want* to stick with you. Be patient. Get to know people. It will become clearer and clearer which ones are meant to be life-long friends.

Don't be afraid to revisit friendships that don't feel good any-more. People grow, they evolve, they change the way they treat themselves and others. Sometimes you learn that someone you thought was a friend wasn't really a friend to begin with. You may find that a childhood friend made sense in the simpler world of childhood, but didn't translate so well to the complex world of adulthood. Sometimes you discover that the way someone treats others in their life bothers you, and that you don't want that energy in your life. These feelings are all okay to have. I've had some of them myself. Be true to who you are and how you feel, and be respectful if and when you part ways.

In this day and age of "liking" and "friending" the multitudes on social media sites, the value of real friendships is priceless.

I say to Daddy all the time, "I hope Hartley has really good friends." I'm your mama, and because of that, I will always want you surrounded by loving, caring, honest, warm, authentic people you can count on. I can't wait to get to know your friends and to welcome them into our family.

My relationships with my close friends are all different. They're each unique and incredible in their own way. With one, I reminisce a lot and plan for future goofball moments. With another, I talk food and family, and we vent about what's bugging us. With yet another, I brainstorm creative ideas. The really good friends in your life will each enhance your life in different ways. You'll reach for the phone to call them at different times, but they will all be a gift.

When you find those good friends who bring you endless laughter and unconditional love and support, treasure them.

Take care of the people in life who take care of you.

I love you more than life,
Mama

Back Up on the Backup Plan

Dear Hartley,

Eventually, no one will know you better than *you*. You'll try different things, you'll have lots of experiences, and then one day, you'll realize you have a decision to make about what you want to do with your life. There will be plenty of people around you with plenty of opinions, but only you can decide what is best for you.

Sometimes I did that well.

I chose a local college over a more prominent university because my visit to that local college felt right. Great choice. I loved those years.

I cut short a PhD program at an Ivy League school, and ended my time there with a master's degree instead, because I found the environment of the school cold and stifling. Great choice. I spared myself years of being cooped up in stuffy, impersonal classrooms focused on a topic of study that wasn't my calling.

I left a job that I was finding less and less rewarding and got into television. Great choice. I love television, I love being on television, and I'm on the right path to develop content I'm passionate about.

I met a man I cared deeply about and married him, even though a few people thought he was too young for me. Great choice. Now I have the best life partner a woman could ask for and you have a wonderful father.

But there were other times I didn't make the right choices for myself.

For most of my childhood, I wanted to be an actress. I was always reenacting scenes from television or making up skits at friends' houses to keep us entertained. I wasn't a singer or a dancer, but I liked acting and felt like I was pretty good at it. There was just one problem: I was painfully shy.

Your grandma taught performing arts to kids in our living room when I was growing up. I sat in on improvisation classes and monologue coaching for fun. It felt comfortable for me to disappear into someone else's life, to keep my focus on their problems, not mine. I had a great love for film and television.

So, what happened?

Well, for one thing, I started to share with others that I wanted to act. I got a lot of: "You need a backup plan." Over and over and over again. I found it really hard to tune that stuff out. Grandpa, a very practical guy as you will come to see, wasn't the adventurous type when it came to career pursuits. Impractical journeys make him nervous. He likes the idea of steady, reliable salaries and job security. "Acting is fun," he would say. "But what are you *really* going to do?"

I remember one disagreement in particular where I said to him, "You wouldn't dissuade another kid if they wanted to be an actress!"

"I would if they were serious!"

That one stuck with me. I remember that he apologized afterward because he saw my face sink when he said it and immediately knew he had made a mistake. Grandpa wasn't trying to hurt me. He was worried that I'd spend my life trying to make something happen that would always be just out of reach.

What he didn't understand was that, for me, life would always be about reaching, so I may as well be reaching toward something I love.

Regardless, his words stuck. I spent my young adult years working toward that "backup plan."

As I mentioned, high school was rigorous for me. It was academics all day, every day at St. Joseph Hill Academy High School, a private, all-girls Catholic school. I was up super early to study before school daily, and I worked hard all day in school and after school, often studying straight up until 10:00 p.m. The weekends were no different. All of my electives were, well, not fun. Advanced Placement Calculus was one of my senior electives. I didn't like math, but I knew the class would read well on a high school transcript. I can't remember the rest of my electives, but they all sounded like classes one would be forced to take, not opt to take. My "fun" activity was the yearbook committee. I applied to be literary editor and got the job. Again, a decision made with my transcript in mind. I spent hours upon hours editing yearbook content. I didn't have much fun. Even the clubs I joined were added to my schedule with my transcript in mind. I was always thinking about how a college review board would see it all.

I wanted a college scholarship. I needed a college scholarship. Grandma and Grandpa had saved up money for my schooling, but I wanted my brain to help pay for it. I became so focused on a "backup plan" and the demanding academics that would help secure it, that the thing I really loved to do, acting, just drifted away. It got drowned out by exams, grade obsession, and submission timelines.

To her credit, Grandma had pushed for me to go to a different high school. She wanted me to go to Staten Island Academy, a co-ed school on the Island that gave students room to figure themselves out beyond academics. The school had lots of clubs, social gatherings, and plenty of space in the schedule to, well, breathe. I had chosen Hill primarily because I was super shy and all of my friends were going there. I wasn't quite ready to start over and make new ones.

I left high school with a lot of learning under my belt and a fantastic transcript. But, and this is a big BUT, I had no idea who I was. More than that, I had lost myself in the midst of burying my head in schoolbooks all day and night.

I wanted to fix it.

I was determined to fix it.

At that point, my close friends from Hill were going to New York University. I had been accepted there, but I visited the campus and didn't like it. I don't know why, but it didn't feel like the right fit for me. I went to see a dorm one day, this tiny dark room with a small window that overlooked some crazy construction. It was so loud. I felt the pull of my friends toward NYU and the familiarity that would come with that choice, but I resisted.

I visited Wagner College that same week, a local college on Staten Island. I sat in on a psychology class in Main Hall, this big, beautiful building that looked like an old church. In a corner room on the second floor, I alternated between listening to the professor and looking out the open window to the trees and grass outside. Something about that place felt like me. So I made my first big move to fix my high school mistakes and went to the college I wanted to go to.

That was my first consequential attempt at self-determination.

It was a home run. I loved Wagner College. I had an amazing four years, met two of my best friends there, and fell in love for the first time. I even picked an unconventional major, Spanish literature. I remember Grandma asking, "What will you do with that?" But I had a plan. I'd complete a business minor to leave my options open, then apply to grad school for a PhD in Spanish so that I could teach it at the college level.

Did I like teaching? Well, no, not really. Did I want a career in the business world? Well, no. But I had a plan, right? That counted for something?

Not always, Hartley. A plan makes sense for you only if the plan actually...makes sense for you.

I was still living inside the safety net and didn't even realize it. Sure, I had branched out and chosen a school my friends didn't pick. That was a step. I had even picked Spanish as my major when no one around me seemed to understand that choice. I also found myself in a completely impractical relationship, from which I learned so much about love and life. I had taken a leap there too. But when it came to a job, career, or life path, those two words—backup plan—were still with me.

I worked hard to get a 4.0 GPA (perfectionist tendencies don't die easily), was the class valedictorian, studied abroad, and left with a full fellowship to study at Columbia University for a PhD in Spanish literature.

Eager to compete at the highest level of academia, I had chosen Columbia over Boston College and Rutgers, both of which also offered fellowships. Your grandparents were so proud. There was something about my academic success that really made them beam. Grandpa, in particular, filled a wall in our house with my academic awards. There was a part of me that always wondered if he would've displayed an Emmy or an Oscar quite as proudly. I'm still not sure.

Columbia was a great idea as far as ideas go. Ivy League, best of the best, intense New York City environment, deep history of academic excellence, exposure to world-renowned experts in the field. It would look great on my résumé and set me on a path for high-level achievement in academia and a respected career path.

There was just one small problem.

I hated it.

Columbia didn't feel welcoming like Wagner. I was bored and disconnected in my classes. Manhattan made me feel like I was in the wrong place at the wrong time, and I couldn't figure out why. I pushed through for a year, knowing that a Master of Arts from Columbia would mean something. (Would it really, though? To whom?) I think Grandma and Grandpa were a little disappointed when I left the doctoral program. Grandpa thought a PhD would give me professional stability and Grandma joked that it would be cool to refer to me as Dr. Bila. She was joking, sort of, kind of, but not really.

I felt lost again.

I felt that way because I had allowed my backup plan to become my up-front plan. I was now living someone else's dream, not mine.

With my hard-won master's degree in hand, I left Columbia and took a job with an insurance company. I didn't know a single thing about insurance, nor did I want to, but I listened to the voices around me yet again, and opted for stability. The job offered a solid starting salary and a good savings plan.

Then, September 11, 2001.

I was working Downtown at One Liberty Plaza, across the street from the World Trade Center. I missed a note on my desk from my boss asking me to deliver a package to the North Tower by 8:45 a.m. The first plane struck that tower at 8:46 a.m. By that time, I was running for my life in a crowd of scared faces, mine included.

A few days later, grateful to be alive and grieving for those who were not, I made a decision. I was tired of following someone else's prescription for success. I didn't want a predictable life. I wanted an interesting life. I wanted a raw, experimental, follow-your-heart, lived-in kind of life. I was done settling.

Or so I thought.

I waited tables at a restaurant in Rockefeller Center to pay the bills and decided to take some acting classes. I loved them. I excelled. Teachers shared promising words about my work. I remember getting lost in scripts and feeling completely found. Could I do this acting thing? Was my time *now*? And then, some opinions came my way:

"You're twenty-three. You're too old to start. It's not like you did *The Mickey Mouse Club* or anything."

"You have a degree from Columbia. Why waste your time with this stuff?"

"Acting? You'll be one in a zillion."

"Shouldn't you have some film credits by now? I mean, aren't you a bit late to the party?"

I vowed to tune it all out. I did some showcases. I booked some local commercial work. I even went out to Los Angeles for a few weeks. I had sent my headshot and résumé in for a project and got the audition. I didn't get the job, but I did get an offer for representation. The agent had a roster of auditions lined up for me in Los Angeles. I thought I should extend my visit beyond the few weeks I'd planned.

I called home. And a friend.

"Where will you live?"

"How will you pay rent?"

"What if that agent takes everyone on?"

"Are you going to wait tables? Is that really what you want to do?"

Here's the part where I'll disappoint you, Hartley. I took the bait. Again. I felt mostly alone in the whole process, minus a couple of supportive voices. Even my best friend, who had come to Los Angeles with me for those few weeks, wanted to go home.

So I quit before I even gave it a try.

On my plane ride back to New York, I felt like I was making a huge mistake. I now know that I would be a better person today, a fuller person, a more complete person, if I had at least tried and failed, or better yet, tried and succeeded.

Back in Manhattan, I wandered around, directionless, lost again in my own hometown.

The big irony is that I wound up waiting tables in New York anyway while I figured out my next steps. I actually had a great time doing it because I got to hang out with fun people and dance a lot. I built up my muscles carrying those heavy trays. Co-workers asked why I hadn't just stayed in Los Angeles and waited the tables there while auditioning. I didn't have a good answer. "Because I was a coward" was the truth.

I took a few teaching jobs, one at a Catholic school on Staten Island, then another at a private school on the Upper East Side. I still felt lost.

Then I started writing blogs. One was on politics. I submitted content for consideration to *Runner's World* and a pet magazine, but didn't hear back. As I mentioned earlier, I reviewed a radio host's book and Fox News reached out.

This time, I was brave.

I quit my teaching job to pursue this new TV path. I wasn't getting paid for my TV work right away and had to string together some odd jobs to make ends meet, but the move felt right. TV studios always felt like home. I worked hard and made my way to a small starting salary as a network contributor.

And so my television career began.

These days, I'm not afraid to take a career leap, to say aloud that something no longer serves me or no longer feels right, to take first steps toward opening new doors to new journeys. I'm not afraid to close doors that lead to places I've already been and don't want to revisit.

Be gutsy, Hartley. Sometimes we make the same mistakes over and over before we learn how to fix something in our life that's broken. But you *can* fix it, even if it takes some time.

When it comes to careers, I have no idea what page you'll be on. For all I know, you may choose a stable job with a good 401(k) and stay there for forty years. That's okay, too, as long as it's what you really want to do. It's all about what makes you happy.

No matter what path you choose to follow in life, remember:

Sometimes the struggle is part of the fun.

Don't live a whole life wishing you'd done this or that. Do it. Just do it.

Embrace internal shifts that tell you it's time to make a new move.

Never fear what sounds hard or what people tell you is near impossible. Someone makes it happen and that someone could be you.

I want you to be braver than I was for so many years.

I want you to be able to tell the doubters, "Okay, guys, catch you on the flip side," before you smile and do your best to turn dreams into reality.

Don't dip your toe into the water, Hartley. Jump in, all the way.

Your body may be a little shocked and a lot cold at first, but you'll be swimming toward something you love. That will warm you up.

Forget the backup plan. Live your life like you don't need it.

I believe in you.

I love you more than life,
Mama

Comfy Clothes

Dear Hartley,

It was a gorgeous night in New York City just a couple of months after my twenty-first birthday. It was the first day that really felt like spring, and I had plans to go out with my friend Nicole. Nicole and I were old buddies from middle school and high school.

On this particular night, we were headed to one of the "It" clubs in Manhattan at the time. They had a DJ scheduled whose music I really liked. I knew that he would play not only dance music, but dance music with words. I'm big on lyrics, not only for my love songs, but also for my dance songs.

I bought a great outfit for the night, a little black dress and the best accessory I had ever owned—hot pink, strappy stilettos that were way out of my price range. I had passed them by in a shoe store window for weeks. Finally, I saved up enough money, and a few days before going out, I took the plunge and made the purchase.

These shoes weren't just shoes. These shoes were art.

Dressed and ready to go, I took one last look in the mirror. The outfit was perfect. I was feeling great. This was going to be a night to remember.

Nicole pulled up outside. I walked out of the house, down the steps, along our little pathway to the car, and...

Uh-oh.

Oh no.

The shoes.

Why were they rubbing my toes like that when I walked?

And why did the straps feel like they were digging in when I went down the stairs?

I'd worn them in the store for a few minutes and they had felt okay. But had I even stood up in them? I couldn't remember. They were just so gorgeous, I'm not even sure I strapped them on fully before buying them.

I convinced myself it would all be fine, that I just needed to break them in a little.

We got to Manhattan, found a parking spot a few blocks away from the club, and began our walk there.

My feet were crying.

We stepped into the club. Colorful lights flickered everywhere. My favorite DJ was on fire. Music was pumping my beloved tunes and all I wanted to do was get out there and dance.

But—I couldn't.

I tried, but my shoes were rubbing the skin right off my feet. I mean that quite literally.

To make things worse, my dress started itching. What in the heck was this thing made of, sandpaper?

I was miserable. All I had wanted to do was dance and have fun. Instead, I was stuck trying to dance with burning feet and trying not to scratch my dress off my body. I spent a lot of the night sitting on a lounge chair sulking.

I wish I could say it was unusual for me to make such absurd clothing choices, but unfortunately, I can't tell you how many times I went out in uncomfortable clothes. As I write this, I'm reminded of the time I tore off a wool dress while driving home at night from a friend's house. I'd had it on for only two hours, but my body was beet red and covered in hives. I drove the whole way home in my undergarments and had to call your grandma to meet me downstairs with a robe when I arrived.

I won't even bother getting into the pleather catsuit I once thought would be a great wardrobe option for an outdoor dinner in the middle of a heat wave, but you get the idea.

In an effort to put together a cute clothing ensemble, Mama definitely took a few wrong turns in the comfort department.

In my thirties, I made some pretty big changes in this area, thankfully. I became known as the jeans-and-logo-tee girl. Comfortable jeans, degrees of ripped and weathered, and logo T-shirts, paired with a leather jacket and combat boots in chilly weather or flat sandals in the summer, became my uniform. Your Aunt Lauren and I would venture out to small lounges where they played great retro '90s music and everyone in the room would dance until the morning.

Comfortable clothing made everything better, including my dancing.

After decades of discomfort, I was finally free.

I couldn't remember why I had chosen those uncomfortable clothes to begin with. Maybe it had something to do with my youth. I had worn a school uniform from the time I was in first grade until I graduated from high school. Those knee-high socks, polyester skirts, saddle shoes, and cross ties were not comfortable. Was I just used to uncomfortable clothes and stuck in a cycle of wearing them? Maybe. Even when I got to college, I was oddly compelled to wear uncomfortable items. I would dress up every day for class.

"Jed, where you going, the runway?" my good friend would joke. High-heeled boots, long, fitted skirts, off-the-shoulder, stiff sweaters— I wore it all. I even had sneakers with giant platforms.

Don't get me wrong, I wore comfy clothes at home my whole life, but I had this glitch in my brain about going-out clothes for a long time. My thirties brought lots of sanity to that arena.

Hartley, wear what you feel good in. Wear what you can breathe in. Wear shoes that don't hurt your feet, sweaters that don't itch, and T-shirts that don't have those tags that could drive someone right over the edge. And don't get me started on what happens when you try to cut those tags out. Either you'll be left with some little ridge in there that makes you crazy because it's even itchier than the whole tag was to begin with, or you'll be left with a hole in the fabric where the tag was before you ripped it out in a fit of rage. It's a no-win situation.

Cotton, sewn-in tags? A big win for people everywhere.

Your daddy and I laughed about the horrors of uncomfortable clothes when we first met, as most of our dates were in workout clothes or really casual hangout clothes. He's not a fan of stiff suits, neck-choking ties, or shoes that hurt your feet. Daddy looks amazing in jeans or athletic shorts and a T-shirt, and that's mostly what he wears now when he's not at work or we don't have a fancy event. Even when it comes to his fancier stuff, comfort is his number one.

Now, I'm fully aware that you could become the kind of adult who is 100 percent comfortable in a tuxedo. Maybe you'll wear suits on your days off, for all I know. If that's what you like and feel good in, I'm totally cool with it. Find what works for you and embrace it.

You also may have a job that has a dress code. I've had on-air jobs where the company wardrobe department provided work clothes via a clothing allowance. In those cases, my closet looked like two different people lived in it. One side was filled with clothes provided by work, lots of bright, solid colors and stiffer materials. The other side was my home base—comfy, cozy, and full of earth tones and fabrics your mama could relax in.

Don't be afraid to love your sweatpants, Hartley. I sure love mine.

Also, pay attention to how efficiently you work in different types of clothes. I'm always at my best when I'm comfortable, when I feel most like myself.

And if you ever pass a store and see a pair of overpriced, dazzling shoes that look more like art than shoes, keep on walking.

I love you more than life,
Mama

Outer Spaces

Dear Hartley,

I remember one dinner with a friend where we had a long cultural and political discussion. It seemed like a healthy exchange of ideas and I was happy to hear about her experiences. We agreed on some things, disagreed on others. She even brought me to a new understanding on some issues, and I was grateful for that. I hoped that she felt the same way. Later that night, I received an email from her that said she felt betrayed by some of my views. She had wanted my total, complete agreement on everything. That made me incredibly sad.

The world is a complicated place, Hartley. Consider our country, the United States of America. Hundreds of millions of people live here. One of the most wonderful things about our country is that we are not a homogeneous group of people descended from one specific culture, but rather a diverse lot of cultures and races. That means America is filled with many different people, with many different backgrounds, upbringings, attitudes, ideas, opinions, and worldviews. It's been that way for centuries and I hope it continues to be that way for millennia.

Despite those who sprinkle their nostalgia with a dose of make-believe, America has never been a country of one people united in thought and purpose. Diversity in all of its forms is what has always made our country such a dynamic place to be.

We are living in a time of strange contradiction. On the one hand, we've become a more thoughtful and conscious country when it comes to a lot of diversity-related issues. On the other hand, intolerance to differing views seems to be growing, not shrinking. That concerns me for you and your whole generation. We're creating a more and more divided country, and none of it will change until we fix the way we approach one another, until we accept our differences, welcome real discussions, and recognize that we're not meant to see eye-to-eye on everything. We're meant to help each other think things through.

Factor in social media bullying and trolling, and the situation only gets more complex. The anonymous, and sometimes not so anonymous, adult mean girls and boys on social media apps never seem to get tired. There is an increasing intolerance of differing views in those spaces and a bizarre need to retreat into some echo chamber where people see the world just the way you do. How boring. Then comes a pattern of living in bubbles of homogeneous thought, a more polarized country, and I could go on and on.

Intolerance to dissent is alive and well on both sides of the political aisle. I take some pretty aggressive heat from all corners when I share opinions that don't go-along-to-get-along with the toe-the-line crowds. "Too bad," I say to their complaints. I'm not a toe-the-line kind of gal.

I want you to learn how to engage in a world where people often disagree.

I want you to go to a school that recognizes the importance of free thinking.

I want you to be comfortable hearing both sides of an issue and figuring out where you stand.

I want you to learn from different people with different worldviews.

When someone says something that you disagree with, I want you to tell them why you disagree and talk about it. I want you and them to feel respected and heard. That's how strong people are built. Strong people who have strong conversations and, one day, come up with strong solutions. Together.

I am hopeful that you and your generation will want to make important, positive changes in the way people communicate. I'm hopeful you'll inspire people to abandon their toe-the-line nonsense and start talking to one another.

Embrace thought-provoking books, works of art, and films that get you thinking. When you hear or see something that rubs you the wrong way, think about why you don't like it. Never stop thinking freely.

May you always let the world around you stretch your heart, mind, and soul.

I love you more than life,
Mama

Inner Spaces

Dear Hartley,

My first post-grad-school Manhattan apartment was a small studio that the owner had converted into a one-bedroom so that he could market it that way. It was basically a 375-square-foot room with a wall inserted down the middle. It was super tiny, but the bathroom and kitchen had been gut-renovated, so the place felt small, but new. My living room housed a tiny television stand, a love seat for one, a teeny desk for my laptop, and Bronte's cat bed.

My favorite space in the apartment was underneath a window that faced the street below. The view outside was nothing special, but it had a feeling of old-time New York. Maybe that had something to do with the beautiful building across the way that I often stared at from that window. From my little space on the third floor, I could hear the click-click of shoes on the pavement below, the intermittent honking of taxis, and the breathless chatter of children running down the street.

I was content and comfortable in my little space.

I had set up the small desk with an even smaller chair just beneath the window. On the window's ledge, I had initially placed an adorable little cactus plant. That went well until Bronte hissed at it and knocked it over. I replaced the plant with a photo of me, Grandma, and Grandpa in Paris, from a trip we took to France and Belgium when I was sixteen. It was one of the best trips I've taken in my life. We ate delicious food, saw incredible architecture, and ate more delicious food, while laughing nonstop. To this day, the smell of Belgian waffles transports me.

Many days when I was teaching, I would come home to that small apartment feeling tired. I was sometimes a little sad because I felt like I wasn't following my passion. Teaching was fun and there were a lot of great lessons to be learned from doing it, but I wasn't in my zone and I knew it. Once I opened the door to that little apartment, though, I would feel completely at peace, full of hope that my cozy abode would restore my energy and renew my optimism. Immediately, I would be drawn to the little chair beneath the window, the special space I had made for myself. There, I would read, write in my journal, call a friend, or just sit, look out the window, and dream. Bronte would jump up onto my lap and fall asleep while I got lost in reading, writing, or talking.

I have always made it a priority to create inviting spaces for myself in the places I've lived, whether it was my bedrooms growing up, my apartments in Manhattan and Brooklyn, or our home right now. My graduate school bedroom had a really cool loft bed. I would climb a small ladder to get up there for long phone conversations.

In our home now, I've taken over a little corner of Mommy and Daddy's bedroom. It has a cushy brown velvet chair that I love to sink into. It's where I cozy up with my thoughts. Late at night, in this corner, I think and write.

The spaces we live in have the capacity to really affect how we feel. I hope you create your own special spaces in the places you live throughout your life. I want you to have a quiet, comfy spot in your apartment or house that is all your own, a spot to think, recharge, and feel the weight of the day lift off your shoulders.

It always helps me to place something extra special in those already-special spaces, like a little trinket with sentimental value or a photo I love. In our home now, I have a little shelf near my cushy chair in the bedroom. On that shelf sits an action sign, one of those black-and-white signs you see on film sets that mark the start of a scene. It fills my heart to see it because it makes me think of the television and film sets I love so much. It reminds me of goals I have that might be just within reach. Right beside that sign stands a small photo of you, smiling while at the playground. Your face lights me up.

Around our home, we also have items that brighten our days. We have pictures of me, you, and Daddy blown up on canvases on the walls. In our bookcases, we have baby pictures of you and some wild engagement and wedding photos that our friend Jordan Matter took of Daddy and me. Jordan is an unconventional photographer, so he had us climbing fences, dancing in the middle of the street, and running through a snowstorm. His photos are all kinds of beautiful craziness. I also stuck a fun blown-up photo of me and Sunny Hostin in one of our hallways. Sunny co-hosted *The View* with me and is still one of my pals. To launch the twentieth season, the co-hosts made a Mary J. Blige music video and used the song for our show's theme. In the photo, Sunny and I are popping our heads out of a door, smiling. We laughed all day that day, and when I look at that photo, I can't help but smile thinking of us taping those scenes.

On a small ledge downstairs, we have two dice to remind us to be spontaneous, roll the dice, and see where they fall. We also have an hourglass bookend that reminds me of watching *Days of Our Lives* with my grandma, and all of the hopes and dreams that went with those afternoons. We've hung a copy of *The Son of Man* painting by René Magritte in our kitchen, because Grandma hung one in our home when I was little. At first, as a kid, I was scared of it, until Grandma made up a funny story that it was Grandpa in the painting, with an apple in front of his face. Ever since then, I've just liked having that painting around. It's been with me since my very first apartment.

We also have a tiny plaque on the downstairs desk that says "Love you to the moon and back" because that's what your daddy and I used to say to each other when we met, and still do. Of course, now, we also say it to you.

Warm, comforting spaces make all the difference, Hartley.

Let the spaces you love and the meaningful things you place in them lift you up on tough days.

Let them help you celebrate wonderful ones.

Let them remind you of where you've been and excite you for where you're going.

I love you more than life,
Mama

Balance

Dear Hartley,

Manhattan. Circa 2003. I'm in a lounge Downtown with some friends. It's dark, the chatter is loud, the music is even louder, and the bartenders and cocktail waitresses are moving quickly to satisfy a thirsty crowd. I'm talking with my friends and dancing, when out of the corner of my eye, I see someone looking at me with a really angry expression. I look away, then back a couple of times. She's still staring. And then, suddenly, something's hurling fast toward my face. It's a...*fist? What? What's going on here?*

That girl was twice my size, and she was taking a solid swing at me for no particular reason. Or maybe there was a reason and I just didn't know it, and still don't. Perhaps I looked like someone she knew and didn't like so much. At any rate, she went right for my face, my right cheek actually. The thing was, she had terrible balance. I ducked and sidestepped the punch, staying on my feet while she fell forward into the crowd behind me.

Good balance. It changes everything.

I've always worked on my balance. I used to lift weights while standing on BOSU training balls, air-box with my eyes closed, and do plenty of exercises on one leg to promote a strong core and stability. I even trained for a short time with a guy at a Lower Manhattan boxing gym who got me to anticipate his moves and react without losing my balance. I liked balance work because it made me feel strong and centered.

The word "balance" is pretty far-reaching. There's the physical balance we just talked about, but there are other kinds too.

Daddy and I strive to balance our work, while alternating taking care of you and Daisy.

Sometimes you have to balance doing the stuff you love with doing the stuff that pays the bills, hoping that one day the two will unite and become one.

Finding balance in life isn't always easy. But we all have to do it.

If and when you find yourself in an unexpected predicament that involves your body or mind, plant your feet on the ground, find your balance, get centered, and, if necessary, duck.

I love you more than life,
Mama

Tumbles

Dear Hartley,

Even though I pride myself on having good balance, your mama tumbles sometimes too. Yesterday I found myself lunging through the air after tripping on the slightly protruding edge of your high chair. Once, I slipped on a banana peel outside in Manhattan and landed halfway in a garbage pail, right there in plain sight on Lexington Avenue. Oh yeah, and there was that time I tripped over Daisy, knocked into your daddy's smoothie, and we all found ourselves in a puddle of raspberry-blueberry deliciousness.

Like I said, there have been some tumbles. And there's a big reason why.

Mama rushes. It seems like there are always five hundred things to do in a day. Twenty-four hours just isn't enough time. And so, I hurry here and hurry there. I hurry to unload groceries, to fold clothes, to feed Daisy, to get some exercise, to take a shower. I don't like to rush my time with you, so I rush around when you're napping, when you're with Daddy or Grandma or Grandpa, or after you go to bed.

Bottom line: I need to stop rushing so much.

That's not easy for me to do. I have one of those minds that races. I make mental lists of things to do, and just when I finish something, another chore pops into my head that I just have to get done. I'm a doer. Always moving, always cleaning, always thinking, always doing...something.

I constantly have to remind myself to slow down. Intellectually, I know that rushing around is bad. Luckily, I do generally have good balance and haven't hurt myself yet, but it's not rocket science to conclude that you're more likely to fall if you're rushing.

It's also bad for our minds to rush so much. I believe in meditation, relaxation, finding inner peace, and yet, here I am, in between all of those healthy choices, rushing around as if someone has hit the fast-forward button on me. That's not good. I want to change that bad habit. I want to lead by example and show you that I *can* change it. I want to show you that we can all make positive changes if we put our minds to it.

Rushing around like crazy, only to roll into a tumble, is not something you need to do. Give yourself a few extra seconds to get where you need to go. I want you to give your mind more of a consistent sense of calm than I have given mine.

But I also want you to learn a more important lesson: We're all a work in progress. I'm not writing this book as some perfect end product who made mistakes in the past, but now has it all figured out. I'm writing it as someone who has made great strides in some areas, but still has plenty of work to do in others. I'm learning, just like you. And growing, just like you. It will always be this way. I promise to share the things I got wrong and figured out, as well as the things I got wrong and still struggle with. Maybe one day you can help me do better at some things too.

That's the plan for me, you, and Daddy—to work together, to be honest with one another, and to help one another with the stuff that challenges each of us.

I'm headed downstairs to see you right now, and my plan is to walk there slowly. Peacefully. No rushing, no tumbling. It's a good start.

I love you more than life,
Mama

Checked Boxes

Dear Hartley,

It's time I told you...

I can't draw a straight line.

Even with a ruler.

I liked to draw as a kid, but I wasn't very good at it. And no, this is not one of those situations where one might wonder: *Were you really just an up-and-coming artist unappreciated in your time?* Nope. Drawing wasn't part of my natural, God-and-universe-given abilities. Even my tracing, following the lines of an object sitting right there on the page, needed some help. Still does.

It wasn't a big deal to me to be bad at drawing when I was young, because in elementary and middle school, we weren't graded on the quality of our drawings, but instead just given credit for completing the assignments. That worked for me. I'm an achievement kind of gal. Give me a task, tell me how to complete it, and I'm there. I was always worried about my grades, so when you took grading out of the artistic equation, I instantly calmed down.

Getting good grades was at the forefront of my mind in high school because I wanted and needed that college scholarship. Once in college, I continued to focus on good grades, my eyes on graduate school fellowships. Grandma and Grandpa had saved up money for my schooling, but some college and university expenses were, and are, just outrageous. My parents couldn't possibly cover it all.

When I got to college, I created a formula for myself:

Take classes I knew I would do well in + work hard = get good grades.

Check, check, check.

But part of me itched to do something new. To try something, dare I say, experimental. So I did.

My first bold move was to take an introduction to acting class, and I loved it. I did well, received great feedback from the teacher, and was satisfied with my A. But let's be honest, taking acting hadn't really been that bold or experimental for me. Acting was something I felt I was pretty good at, so it was a safe kind of bold.

One day, my advisor told me about a class called Introduction to Studio Art. Other students I knew were talking about it, about how fun and relaxing it was. I'd never known a class to be relaxing, and I thought that after thirteen years of intense schooling, I deserved a little relaxation.

The class met in a beautiful room with giant windows. People seemed so calm as they approached their easels. Throughout the lesson, there was a lot of friendly chatter. I'd never seen anything like that. Talking? During class? That was new, for sure. I was excited to try it all out.

The first day, we drew circles. Just circles. That was the whole assignment.

I stepped back, considered my work, assessed the work of those nearby, and with all the honesty of the most astute critic, decided that my circle...stunk.

It was bad. Really bad. It looked like it had been stretched out, or maybe it was crooked. Or maybe it was stretched out and crooked. Shouldn't I have mastered circles in kindergarten?

The next class, we did squares. Again, I stepped up to the easel and crafted a shape with what I envisioned to be proper horizontal and vertical dimensions. Again, I stepped back and took a look. My square...stunk. And it was also crooked.

This pattern continued. I'd get an assignment, step up to the easel, draw something, step back, and...ugh.

Now, I realized I had a tendency to judge myself harshly. I was highly critical. But I just couldn't shift my perspective. I was always left disappointed with what I had produced. That disappointment took the fun right out of the whole experience and made it anything but relaxing. It actually induced anxiety. Worse, none of my shapes looked worthy of an A. They were more in the B or C zone. I started to worry.

The irony was that a lot of the other students had taken that class to get an easy B. I just couldn't let go of my perfectionist tendencies. I was consumed with grades, grades, grades. An A in this art class was far from a sure thing.

My teacher tried to encourage me to stay, but I wasn't having it. I dropped the class and replaced it with upper-level art history. That class required intensive study, trips to museums, research, essays, and the writing of a big, long, meticulously footnoted final paper.

This, I could handle. This, I knew how to do.

This whole line of thinking was a mistake, Hartley. Sure, I got an A in the art history class, but it wasn't satisfying. The journey wasn't new or bold or experimental. It was predictable. In dropping the

studio art class, I had lost the chance to learn how to navigate something outside of my comfort zone, to open up a new and different
part of my brain, and to just have fun. I had also missed the chance
to learn that it's not all about the A's.

I missed all of that because I was so programmed for academic
study that I couldn't figure out how to do anything but study. A class
spent drawing circles and squares was mysterious and intriguing,
but for a girl so focused on grades, it was also downright scary. I
would've been more at ease calculating the geometry of those shapes
than drawing them.

A year or so later, I found the guts to venture off the academic
path once more. Ruminating on romantic visions of Demi Moore
and Patrick Swayze in the movie *Ghost*, I signed up for ceramics. The
first day, I sat down at the wheel and gave it a literal spin.

That didn't go well.

Nothing would align properly. The clay was a mess. It looked like
a blob of something that had been stepped on accidentally. Once
again, my instructor was very supportive. "Don't worry, it will come
along," the professor said. "You're just getting started." Those words
sounded like a B+ at best. Nope. I couldn't have that. *My transcript
shouldn't have that.* A full fellowship to grad school wouldn't allow
for that.

I was out.

I dropped this class too.

This time, after only a day.

The issue wasn't that I was starting off with no skills in unfamiliar
terrain. I'd done that before. My brain certainly hadn't been naturally wired for AP Calculus or AP Economics, but I had stuck those
out. The reason? There were formulas for those things. There was
memorization and studying. I felt like I could guarantee my success,

or come close to it. But drawing and ceramics weren't like that. They were subjective and boundaryless and I couldn't see a path from A to Z, let alone back from Z to a much-needed A.

I chickened out, living in fear of a less-than-perfect grade that could give me a less-than-perfect future. Or so I thought.

I look back on dropping those two classes with regret. I think about how cool it would have been to make something that I could put a plant in and have in my house. Or to draw something that might not have been the most amazing drawing ever by a long shot, but would have been artistic in its own way, and likely a lot better than I thought I could produce.

Don't get consumed with the A's, Hartley. Don't fill yourself with anxiety over the idea of having to be perfect all the time. No one's perfect. Even those with plenty of A's.

I want you to learn so many things and stretch the boundaries of your brain. I want you to grow a big, beautiful brain. Sure, I want you to do well in school and feel confident in your abilities. But I don't want you to get so caught up in grades and transcripts that it stifles you from venturing into new, challenging, unknown territories. I want you to explore and discover, even if it means you bring home a B instead of an A. That's the only way to really figure out what you like. If any part of you wants to take piano, cooking, woodshop, dance, or anything outside the conventional syllabus, I will completely support that. I don't care what it is. I just care that you'll be unafraid to delve into something new, something a little off the beaten path.

Be braver than I was. Be adventurous with your mind. One day, you will have long forgotten about those grades, but you'll remember those journeys and the things you learned about yourself while taking them.

Do what I couldn't do in college. Try to see the world less rigidly and more fluidly, like this big, exciting, winding path that branches off into interesting detours. Don't be afraid to take as many detours as you want. When you've decided that you're no longer on the right path, look for a new one. It's right there for the taking.

Allow yourself to be as imperfect as we all are, Hartley. Don't fight it, embrace it. Sometimes what you think are imperfections actually wind up being your greatest strengths.

You'll never know what you're capable of unless you try new things. Try it all, even the stuff you think you'll be terrible at. You might be right, but imagine the possibilities if you're wrong.

You're asleep right now while I'm writing this. As I watch you on the baby monitor, I can't help but glow. *I made you*, I think to myself. *Maybe I'm an artist after all…*

I love you more than life,
Mama

Dance Parties

Dear Hartley,

There is a lull in the morning. I've just finished work. Daddy is upstairs folding some laundry. You and I are on the floor, bellies down, playing with an animal puzzle. After several more minutes of semi-quiet concentration on the colorful wood pieces, we both sense it, we both know it.

We need to move.

I get up from the floor, go to my phone, and turn on my favorite playlist. Out from the speaker comes Selena's "Bidi Bidi Bom Bom."

Your head pops up. You listen for a moment, let the rhythm take hold, stand up, and start dancing. Your little legs squat to the melody, a big smile on your face. I step right in to join you, and you smile even bigger.

We love these moments together. You and me, and when Daddy jumps in, we have our dance party of three. Or four, I should say. Because Daisy often runs in circles when we're dancing. Maybe she's dancing too.

You always dance when music starts, from wherever it comes. I adore that about you. And sometimes, when we all have a busy, stressful day, you'll grab your little wooden guitar, bring it over to us, and start pressing musical buttons. It's like you know what we all need. Soon enough, you're smiling and dancing, beckoning us to join. And soon after that, we're all smiling and dancing.

Never change that about yourself, Hartley. No matter what life hands you on any given day, always be ready to turn on some music, find your rhythm, and dance it out.

I love you more than life,
Mama

Empathy

Dear Hartley,

When I was around three and a half years old, Grandma took me to see the movie *E.T. the Extra-Terrestrial*. It's about an alien, a really nice one, that finds itself on Earth and makes friends with a little boy and his siblings. There's a scene in the movie where the alien is dying. He's having trouble breathing, his chest laboriously going in and out, his sweet red heart-light fading...

My chest got tight. *I* had trouble breathing. *What was going on?*

There I was, in the theater, seeing that cute little alien suffering, and I felt like it was happening to me, like I was feeling his pain. Finally, Grandma had to take me out of the theater, get me some fresh air, and calm me down.

To this day, Grandma jokes that, like me, she has never seen the end of *E.T.*

This wasn't just a one-time thing.

When Grandma showed me the animated movie *Charlotte's Web*, I didn't handle Charlotte the spider's impending death so well.

Charlotte's voice sounded all weak and shallow while she was spinning Wilbur's final web, and your mama's voice suddenly felt all weak and shallow...

You get the drift.

Empathy. Feeling what someone else is feeling. Kind of like walking in someone else's shoes and not only understanding their emotions, but feeling them too. That's what was happening to me on those movie-watching afternoons. From the time I was a wee little thing, I was always in touch with the feelings of people and animals around me. Sometimes I felt like I was a little too in touch with it all.

I was the kind of kid who couldn't walk past a pet store without going inside and spending time looking at each and every tenant. I'd beg the store managers to let me hold them so that I could give them some love. I'd be devastated if and when they'd say no. Then I'd spend my whole day trying to figure out how to adopt one or more of them, which is how we got our cat, Scungilli. I would also call people I knew to see if they could adopt any. It got to the point where if Grandma and Grandpa discovered there was a pet store anywhere in sight on our travels, they would drive another way because they knew how much it would upset me.

I felt that kind of empathy for people too. I would sense something was wrong with an adult and step right up beside them to try to figure out what it was. Or if someone was experiencing a great achievement or failure, I would feel the buzz of those sensations right along with them.

I used to think that such a level of sensitivity was a deep flaw. Grandma used to worry that I was going to walk through life with the weight of the world on my shoulders. She has empathy like me, and she knew how hard it was to feel other people's sadness and pain so intensely. I felt their happiness and joy a lot, too, but the sadness and pain were difficult. I wanted to fix things for people I couldn't fix, to help people I couldn't help. It was a lot of emotion for a little person to feel all the time.

As I got older, I realized that empathy was an incredible strength. It has helped me interact with people in powerful ways and affected the way I do my work. When I interview people going through challenges, I come into those conversations with a desire to understand, to feel what they're going through. Whether they've lost a loved one, suffered an illness, or watched their business crumble, empathy facilitates and expands every conversation. It helps me to ask better questions, to get the real story behind the story, and to hopefully make people feel comfortable enough to share what they're going through.

Empathy has made me a better listener, which in turn has made me a better friend, daughter, wife, and mama to you.

Obviously, there are things I will never understand. Any given individual may have gone through a darkness or suffering I can't know. I can try to understand, but sometimes I'll fall short. I'll always have a deep curiosity about the human condition, though.

I remember observing a conversation in my high school cafeteria. Two girls were talking nearby. One was telling a story about her parents not getting along and throwing things at each other in the house. She was clearly upset. The other girl started laughing hysterically, telling jokes about it, even reenacting the story by pulling another girl toward her and throwing food at her. I remember watching the girl who had told the story in the first place, seeing her face drop and lose some color. She tried to laugh along, but it was clear that she was uncomfortable and sad. She had been looking for a different kind of conversation with her friend. I didn't go over to her, as I didn't know her very well, but the look on her face stuck with me.

Empathy is so important, Hartley. Taking the time to feel what people are saying to you and how they're saying it, to consider where they're coming from and how they're feeling in that moment of sharing, makes a big difference. It affects how comfortable they are sharing their struggles with you, and how much better or worse they feel after doing so.

I hope you make the effort to engage people with empathy. It helps them to feel understood. It bonds you to each other in wonderful ways. Your empathy for them may even inspire them to have empathy for you in your times of need.

Empathy generates compassion, inspires kindness, and reminds us of our humanity.

Empathy is a gift you can give to everyone you interact with. It's a deep appreciation for their journey, their story, and the things that make them dim or shine.

Imagine a really hard day. The kind of day that makes you feel hopeless, lost. Your friend is sitting beside you, listening. Think about how you'd like them to treat you in that moment. Consider the empathy you hope they would have for your sadness, fear, or pain.

Be that friend to someone. Be that friend to everyone you can.

I love you more than life,
Mama

Chivalry

Dear Hartley,

Let's say a man opens a door for a woman. Should the woman:

1. Be confused and wait for him to go through first?
2. Consider this is a nice guy doing a nice thing, say thank you, and continue through?
3. Assume that the man thought she was incapable of opening the door herself?

It's all gotten very complicated in 2021.

Some of the complexity has to do with living in a time where gender is a big topic of conversation. Masculinity, femininity, non-binary identifications—these are all terms that we hear often. That's why I want to take the time to discuss a topic that I think gets confused with masculinity, or lumped into the umbrella of masculinity, when it's actually about humanity and involves us all.

That topic is chivalry.

The word "chivalry" is often interpreted to mean how a man acts toward a woman. I think the term should cover more ground than that. I think of chivalry as a kind, respectful, and polite way for any person to act toward anyone else. I think it's less about gender and more about thoughtfulness.

For me, chivalry looks something like this:

Opening doors for anyone, be they man, woman, child, dog, cat, you name it. Not just for your date or your mom, but for the stranger behind you heading into the same store as you, or the person walking out of that store toward you.

Asking someone out in person, face-to-face, not hiding behind a cell phone or some high-tech app. No shields from real exchanges. Lots of eye contact and awkward laughs and all of the good stuff of first encounters.

Picking up the phone to call someone, or getting together with someone in person, if you have something important to say. No texts or emails for the serious stuff like condolences, I'm sorry's, breakups, or "Wanna move in together?" moments.

Calling a no-kill animal shelter when you see a lost dog or cat and staying with them until you can figure out what to do next. Once, when walking with you in your stroller when you were two months old, we saw a tiny puppy tied to a post, barking, wailing. We waited and waited and no owner showed up. Ultimately, we discovered he'd been abandoned and we took him to a no-kill rescue shelter. We got notice that he was adopted just a week later.

Offering to carry packages for anyone who looks like they could use a little help. Of course, they can refuse that help, but I hope you'll always offer. And if you're scolded in the process by someone who's made some crazy assumption about you or society simply because you extended a kind gesture, I hope you brush it off, move along, and offer that same kindness to someone else again anyway.

Daddy and I do kind things for each other all the time. Daddy will offer to carry heavy stuff for me, not because he thinks I can't carry it, but because it's a nice thing to do. He's also stronger than I am when it comes to lifting heavy things, and that's just a fact. I, however, have better balance than he does, so I'll offer to climb up a ladder if we need to, because ladders can get kind of unsteady. Sometimes Daisy, all four pounds of her, will scoot under the tightest furniture or into the tiniest corners to retrieve something for us. Each one of us has an advantage in some area that we can use to help each other out, and when you do that, it's chivalrous.

We've gone a little crazy in our society attributing every little act of kindness to some larger statement about gender or societal oppression or something else.

Sometimes it's just plain kindness, Hartley.

I long for chivalry as we define it in our house, as thoughtful actions and behavior toward everyone, everywhere. For us, it's not about gender, it's about humanity. I hope that you and your generation can bring us back to that.

Don't ever be afraid to spread kindness. And if people are determined to lash out at you, to analyze and overanalyze the simplest of your kind gestures, then know in your heart that perhaps they're the ones who need your kindness most.

I love you more than life,
Mama

Masculinity

Dear Hartley,

The word "masculinity" has gotten a bad name in some circles. Some people feel that it signifies aggression, stubbornness, maybe even oppression.

Perhaps your generation will be the one to redefine masculinity. Or to redefine people's perceptions of it. Maybe a little of both.

Much like chivalry, we have our own brand of masculinity in our home, one that's positive, uplifting, and admirable. Your daddy's masculinity is defined by a lot of things, but a large part of it is the fact that he's an equal partner in taking care of our home and in taking care of you. For me, that's a wonderful masculinity. We both cook, do laundry, clean and maintain the house, feed you and each other. We're both all-hands-on-deck in everything. It's a team, a partnership. I don't even really understand what "traditional male and female roles" are or should be. Nor do I want to. It all sounds pretty limiting and confining, and that's not our style.

Throughout your life, Daddy and I will share with you what we think it means to be a good man.

I think a good man is someone like your daddy. Funny, caring, honest, committed, sensitive, thoughtful, aware.

A good man is a good listener. He's supportive and compassionate.

A good man is kind to animals. In my twenties, I used to say that I would only date guys I would trust to babysit my dog. And I meant it.

A good man is both gentle and strong, cares about his community, and treats people with respect and decency.

A good man embraces you when you've had a rough day and lets you embrace him when he's had a rough one too.

Good men cry when they need to. They laugh, they cry, they give help and ask for help, they inspire and get inspired.

Good men look out for the people they love. When your daddy and I first dated, we went on a lot of long walks together. Daddy always offered to walk me home at the end of the night, because for him, instinctively, that's what felt right.

Your daddy's masculinity is vibrant in everything he does. Many mornings, he'll jump up first to get you out of your crib and give me an extra hour of sleep.

When I was co-hosting a television show remotely from our makeshift in-home studio during the pandemic, Daddy would set up the studio bright and early, then take care of you while I worked, and bring me a homemade snack mid-show. My favorite were his banana pancakes, also now your favorite.

Last night, I was working on a project on the computer. I'm terrible with computer stuff, but Daddy's great with technology, so he rushed to help, as he always does. He's a "What can I do to make your day better?" kind of guy.

Daddy and I make a good team. We gravitate toward different aspects of caring for you.

When I'm in need of a thirty-minute exercise break to clear my head, he's the first to encourage me to take it while he brings you to the park or to Grandma's to play.

On the rare occasion that I have to take a long drive without Daddy, he checks in on me, calling to make sure I'm okay.

He even does things he absolutely doesn't care about just because he knows I care about them. I put small snake plants around our home because I like that they help purify the indoor air we breathe, and sometimes I'll catch Daddy watering them in the kitchen while you eat your snack.

Daddy also takes the time to really look at me when we talk. A short time after we met, I told him, "You have love eyes," because his eyes were always filled with so much tenderness.

And let's not forget your grandpa in all this talk of men and masculinity. Grandpa's a bit old-school, less open than Daddy about his emotions, but sentimental and kind to his core. He has kept every birthday card I ever gave him, and now he keeps all the cute pictures you color for him.

Grandpa has a soft spot for animals and runs around the neighborhood feeding stray cats in the mornings.

When I was little, Grandpa used to walk around our living room with me in his arms, singing "Row, Row, Row Your Boat" to get me to fall sleep.

One night several years ago, he and Grandma were watching one of my favorite movies, *The Notebook*. The story centers around a woman suffering with Alzheimer's. Grandpa lost his own mother to that disease. Grandma said his eyes welled up with tears at the end of the movie, reliving his own family loss.

I'm very lucky, Hartley. I've had a wonderful dad and now have an amazing husband. The men in my life reflect the kind of masculinity I hope you'll come to possess and embrace. It's not built on what society, culture, or the mood of the moment thinks a man should be, but on goodness and many of the traits that help to build a better world.

If you choose a partner one day, I hope you'll be a good teammate, one who is kind and supportive and allows your partner to be kind and supportive in return.

I hope that you and your partner will be invested in your life together, that you will learn to lean on each other and take care of each other.

I hope that you'll be committed to your union in the ways that matter to you both, and that you will be honest about your feelings every day.

It's a powerful thing to be a good man, a good person, and to bring that goodness into the world.

You've already brought me so much joy, my little man. I can't wait to see what's next to come.

I love you more than life,
Mama

Nurturing Nature

Dear Hartley,

This morning, the sun came creeping into our windows with the promise of spring. Your grandma came over, bundled you up in your winter clothes, and took you out for a walk. This is your happy time. You love being outside in quiet areas. You love the stillness, the nature, the peace. You also love to explore, gathering fallen leaves from trees and touching flowers while mesmerized by nearby birds.

I'm so glad that nature nurtures your soul the way it does mine.

For generations, people spent more time outside than inside. Our predecessors worked the land, lived in forests, hunted, farmed, roamed the plains on horseback. The sky, the trees, and the mountains were familiar sights. I often watched a show called *Little House on the Prairie* when I was a kid, and I loved seeing Mary, Laura, and Carrie Ingalls run around the fields all day, spending so much quality time outdoors. Now we are a generation of indoor people. We spend a lot of time inside, whether we're working or relaxing. We miss a lot of the mountains and the streams.

We miss a lot more than that.

We miss the exercise that comes with all of that exploring, the regeneration we feel from sunshine, and the appreciation we gain for things way bigger than us when we see powerful forces of nature at work.

We miss the peace of waterfalls, the gentleness of ocean waves.

So many kids and adults these days spend an abundance of time indoors, tied to our electronics and social media. It's affecting all of us. It's causing us extra stress, making our minds race, and keeping us from a good night's sleep. Spend a couple of hours indoors on your phone, flipping back and forth between emails, social media, and texts. Pay attention to how you feel. Then go outside for a walk without that phone, and breathe in the fresh air while letting the sun shine on your face. Notice the difference in the effect on your body of indoor tech time vs. outdoor tech-free time.

Listen to your body, Hartley. It's always talking to you, trying to help you make better choices by reacting to your choices with symptoms and feelings, both physical and mental.

What I've learned about you in these almost two years of time we've shared together is that you love being outside, and that makes me so happy. I hope that you and your generation find a way to get outside. A lot. I hope the outdoors is your textbook, at least one of them.

Look up at the stars at night.

Make snow angels in the snow, jump in and out of rain puddles, and take long walks on sandy beaches.

There are miracles all around us in nature with so many lessons to teach. And so much power to heal.

As I write this, you're at the park with Daddy, and he just called to tell me you're doing one of your favorite things, tossing food to the birds. He says you're smiling the biggest smile.

May you always know the joy from nature that you know today.

I love you more than life,
Mama

Leading from Within

Dear Hartley,

I think a lot about education. I think about it more now that I have you, now that I've begun to envision what schooling could look like for you. Teaching middle school, high school, and college helped form some of my perspectives on education. But a lot of my feelings about it came from just living.

My own education had some holes in it that I wish had been filled. I made some choices that I wish I had made differently.

Let's start with middle school and high school...

I spent most of my math classes in middle school and high school memorizing formulas. I had been given no real-life context in which to use those formulas and wound up having all of this stored information that I could apply in only very limited ways, because I didn't really understand what I was doing. I used to call Grandpa from the racks at a clothing store so he could figure out the sale price of a sweater because I never learned how to actually think a math problem through. Once a real-life math example would appear before me, without a textbook or standard equation, I was lost. I couldn't apply what I had learned because I hadn't learned, I had memorized.

Grandpa, who grew up in a generation where people actually learned to think, can do 15 percent of 548 in about a second and answer questions like "If Fred leaves the store at ten o'clock and Sally leaves at noon and they walk around the block four times, how soon will they walk into each other?" I remember studying for my GRE, the standardized test you take to get into graduate school, and there was an analytical section that was full of math problems like the example I just gave you with Fred and Sally. I opened up my GRE prep book the first day I got it, read one of those problems, and thought, *Huh?* I showed Grandpa, he lowered his glasses, thought about it for a second, and said, "Oh, five. Yeah, that would be five."

Huh?

He was right. He had figured out the answer. Because he was thinking. He didn't have a formula. He just had his own brain. I realized that somewhere along the line, I had found a false sense of security in formulas. I had learned to trust them instead of trusting my own thought process. I was intimidated by plain old thinking when it came to math. And that was bad. Plus, I had completely missed the fun part of figuring stuff out. To me, it had all become about the formula, the right answer, the grade. I spent a lot of time in my middle school and high school classes, particularly in the math and science areas, focusing on memorizing instead of reasoning.

I hope that your grade school is a place where you learn how to think and reason things through. I want you to learn how to write (luckily, that *was* prioritized in my school) and how to use your own logic to navigate to a solution. I'd even rather you get an answer wrong and be able to reason almost all the way through it, than get it right and have no idea how you got the answer or what it means.

I hope your middle school is a place where you have the chance to explore different areas, some academic and others more creative and athletic. I hope you get to ask lots of questions and learn how to gather information, be it from indoor research or outdoor projects.

I hope your high school is a place where your opinion is respected and heard, even if you feel differently from your teacher or other students. I hope that you learn the importance of listening before reacting to someone else's words.

I hope you get the chance in high school to figure out what you really like. I went to such an intense high school academically, but I left there with no idea what I was passionate about. My school didn't prioritize self-discovery, and that wasn't good for me. Grandma had been reluctant to send me to that high school for that very reason, and she had been right. Of course, I had been stubborn and wanted to go where I wanted to go, and she gave in. My guess is that she regrets that a little. I'm going to try to find an atmosphere for you where education and self-discovery go hand in hand, and I hope you'll strongly consider the value in that.

If I could do it again, Hartley, I'd choose a high school that offered ceramics and woodworking, taught me how to build something like a chair or a bench, had an electronics class where I could fix an appliance or a device, took our class outside to plant a garden and grow some food, showed us how to change a flat tire. Education shouldn't just be about grades or test scores. It should also be about real-life learning and real-life skills. It should be about helping to build a whole person.

One of my politics teachers in high school inspired us to really think. She gave us the tools to passionately disagree with her and one another. She felt she had done a good day's work if we learned how to discover our own truths and felt supported by her in that process. Interestingly enough, that teacher recently attended a lecture of mine and we had a great back-and-forth debate. It was wonderful. I know that she knows I can only do that because she taught me, at a very impressionable age, that respectfully speaking my mind and accepting challenges to my own way of thinking were the only ways to grow up and learn something. I hope that by the time you graduate from high school, you've been through a system, conventional or otherwise, that gives students a chance to think for themselves, to think critically, to think thoughtfully, to think at all. That one teacher I had was monumental in my life, but she was just one. I wish there had been more like her.

When it came to college, I had a great experience. College was where I learned how to speak and write in a second language, how to appreciate and analyze art and literature, how to build lasting friendships, and how to love with my whole heart. But I'd be lying if I said I didn't worry about some aspects of college today. College needs to be a place where free thinking is welcomed and nurtured, where people with all different kinds of opinions come together to talk, debate, grow, and figure out what they believe in. Those different viewpoints need to have a seat at the table. That debate needs to be fostered. If not, college has completely lost its way and its purpose. Of course, we'll have to take this one day at a time and see what the college experience looks like when you're older. And hey, if you decide that college isn't for you, and that you'd prefer a trade school to pursue a particular field or skill you love, Mama and Daddy will support you in that too. There are so many educational paths out there, and there will likely be even more by the time you're older. I'm hoping we can arrive at the best option for you together.

Hartley, your daddy and I will cheer you on as you pursue your education, whatever form it takes. And we will be involved. We will be aware of what you're learning and what you're not, guiding you as you make decisions, and offering lessons learned from the good and bad choices we made in our own schooling. Parents and guardians are essential in this process. School can be hard, and it's a lot for kids to deal with. Take a look behind the curtain of the best students and you'll likely see a supportive family member or family friend ready to help. Teachers work long hours, focused and intent throughout the day, as do school guidance counselors. Those hardworking teachers and counselors need parents and guardians to be active participants in the whole process. Kids stand to gain so much from that.

When education is done right, we give our children the chance to be their best, to become responsible, self-reliant, resourceful, creative, independent-thinking people.

To have the confidence to not look for easy answers.

To learn skill sets that actually help them in the real world.

To be outspoken in the defense of their beliefs, and outspoken in the defense of others' rights to disagree with their beliefs.

To embrace complexity of thought and a peaceful, robust exchange of ideas.

To discover leadership from within.

I hope this all happens for you as you grow into your education. You're getting so big, so fast. Before we know it, it will be time for school of some kind. Daddy and I promise to do our very best to choose for you, and later choose *with* you, educational environments where you can really grow, each and every part of you.

I love you more than life,
Mama

Umbrella Man

Dear Hartley,

As usual, I'm in a hurry. I grab my bag, jacket, and put on my boots. Daddy is at work. I have two appointments down the street and I'm leaving you with Grandma and Grandpa for a bit.

"It might rain," your daddy says over the phone.

I glance over at my umbrella. I'll be gone just a few hours. I don't give it a second look.

"Okay," I answer. I hang up, give you one last kiss, and head out the door.

My first meeting goes fine and, as expected, I'm walking to my second appointment thirty minutes later. Suddenly, darkening clouds, a quick shift of wind, a few drops of rain, and then, the downpour of wet. I'm caught. No hat, no umbrella, a light jacket. By the time I slide into the lobby of my destination, I'm sopping wet. Soaked. My hair is a matted mess. My clothes are clinging.

Needless to say, I do not make my best physical impression.

Your daddy refrains from an *I told you so* when I call him, but I can hear it in his voice. Then he begins to laugh hysterically because he's looking at the photo I sent him of me looking like I'd just gotten off a water ride.

Hartley, make your life easier. Check the weather. Bring an umbrella.

I realize that you may be a lot like me and resist this simple act of practical preparation, but don't. Or at least try not to. Real-life rainy days don't look like they do in the movies. You won't romantically strut down the avenue, tiny droplets illuminating your face while you spontaneously stumble upon a long-lost friend. Instead, you'll just get wet. Sometimes really, really wet.

Unlike Mommy, Daddy checks the weather. If it says it's going to rain, he grabs an umbrella. He stays dry, which keeps him happy. It's so simple.

Daddy even stores an umbrella in the car for us now, which I discovered the last time I got stuck in torrential rain and he said, over the phone, these magical, heavenly words: "There's an umbrella in the back seat."

Believe me, I get spontaneity. I get the charm of "I'm going to leave the house, live in the moment, and embrace whatever the day brings." Your mama is the queen of wanting to find movie-style moments in everyday life.

There's a great time and place for those romantic thoughts, the ones that leave you open to new adventures. But getting caught in the rain and going into a meeting sopping wet isn't one of them.

Sometimes life is simple, it's raining, and you just need an umbrella.

I love you more than life,
Mama

Back to the Future Fuel

Dear Hartley,

When I was a kid, I was a candy junkie.

Grandma was, and is, a great cook and put an abundance of delicious homemade food on the table every night for dinner. She'd also pack me a good, wholesome lunch. But when I was at school or at friends' houses, I ate a lot of junk food—chips, candy, frosted cereals, and basically any garbage food I could get my hands on. We also always had some cake and cookies at home and I'd eat too much of them, too often, because I had a wicked sweet tooth. I did this as often as I could get away with, and I continued this behavior right on through college.

In my junior year of college, I developed acid reflux. That's a troublesome condition where your stomach acid makes its way back up into the esophagus, the tube of muscle that brought the food down in the first place. It can be degrees of irritating (mine was pretty bad) and can feel like it's hard to breathe. I took some prescription medication and it helped at first. Doctors talked to me very vaguely about diet, like avoiding spicy foods and foods with too much acidity, but the medication was their primary recipe for "healing." Guess what happened to me? Soon enough, I couldn't eat anything without the medication.

This lasted for four more years. YEARS. It would go from horrible to mildly horrible to bad to okay to horrible again, cycling over and over. One time I even called an ambulance because I thought I was having an allergic reaction and my throat was closing. Turns out it was just the reflux creating swelling and inflammation. The doctors gave me more medicine. It didn't get better.

I was talking about it with your Aunt Lauren one night, when she said, "Have you read that book *Eat to Live?*"

I hadn't, but I ordered it right after we hung up. I read it, highlighted it, even went out to New Jersey to see the doctor himself and discuss what was going on. I was blown away by what I heard.

I soon learned what I now know all too well:

What we put into our bodies matters. Big-time.

Since your mama is a woman of immediate action, I made changes quickly. I shifted my habits that very day. I figured, *Well, nothing else has worked, so let's give this a try.* I got rid of processed foods. Basically, any finished product you could buy in a box had to go. I also went full-on plant-based, which means I didn't consume foods derived from animals. I ate lots of organic fruits and vegetables, salads, homemade soups, and raw nuts. As it turned out, a lot of the advice the traditional medical establishment had given me about foods to avoid had been wrong. In fact, sometimes it was the complete opposite of what worked for me.

I changed what I ate for a full month. I ate all whole foods. Nothing processed, nothing fast. Juicing became a go-to way for me to get my nutrients. I studied which fruits and vegetables were good for juicing and for me. I blended organic fruits and vegetables into smoothies. I started feeling better. I had a lot of energy too. I began adding supplements to my diet, and not just any supplements, but high-quality supplements built from whole foods.

The next thing I knew, my acid reflux disappeared. Completely. I was eating lots of nuts and raw vegetables, adding red pepper to soups. These had all been foods the traditional medicine doctors had told me to avoid. Here I was, eating them with not an ounce of reflux.

I couldn't believe it. I couldn't believe that changing the food I consumed could have such a big impact on my body so quickly. I didn't only feel better, I felt great.

Throughout the years, I would go through cycles where I would bring meat back in, then take it out again. But I became very attuned to the quality of meat, seeking out organic, grass-fed meats, wild fish, and organic poultry, all from farms or markets where I knew the sources well. If I wanted something sweet, I didn't reach for processed cake mix in a box. Instead, I would use ingredients like fresh oats, almond butter, bananas, and dark chocolate to bake something delicious from scratch. If I wanted pizza, I would make it at home using high-quality ingredients. It tasted as good as what we had at the pizzeria and way better than any frozen pizza from the store.

A few years later, I got a knockout punch that pushed my wellness regimen to a whole new level. It involved a quick getaway and a ridiculous relationship I was in...

One summer weekend, I went out to the Hamptons Beaches on Long Island, New York. I had never been there before. A friend of my then-boyfriend had a house there and we were going to stay two nights. By that point, my relationship was already a mess, but I was romantically chasing the clouds, looking for the silver linings and trying to revive it.

After that weekend of sun, pool time, some arguments, and not as much fun as I'd hoped for, I got home and noticed a small stamp-like rash on my leg. It was circular, sort of, and oddly specific in its boundaries, well-defined. It didn't itch or hurt, wasn't puffy. It was a Sunday, so I decided I'd call my doctor on Monday if it still looked odd. By the next day, it was mostly faded. The following day, it was gone completely. I figured it was nothing.

A couple of weeks later, I had a night where I sweat right through my pajamas and all over the bed. I thought I was getting sick, but I didn't feel sick. It was very strange.

Fast-forward a few months, and I was tired. All the time. My legs felt heavy. More than tired, I was fatigued, even from just walking around my apartment. This was weird for me, Hartley. I was the kind of person who ran to the gym, worked out, ran home from the gym, then hit a few push-ups and sit-ups back at the apartment for good measure. Now I was suddenly filled with exhaustion, even when I was just sitting around watching a movie.

So I went to the doctor. She did some standard blood work, and a few days later told me it all looked fine. She suggested that I had too much on my plate, that I was just overworked. She said I should try to get more rest.

A month later, I was still fatigued. I remember one night, in my studio on the Upper East Side, I was watching television (reruns of *Dawson's Creek*, I'm pretty sure) when I suddenly felt a numbness and tingling in my right cheek. Then it went away. Wait, no, there it was again. Then the whole right side of my face felt oddly stiff. I kept moving my face around, thinking, *Have I lost my mind? Is this feeling real?* It was very odd. Very random. And very creepy.

I made an appointment with the doctor again and insisted that something was wrong. "I know my body," I kept saying. "You're missing something."

She ran more tests.

I got a call a few days later.

"We found it. You have Lyme disease. But don't worry, the numbers show that we caught it early."

Lyme disease? I knew that term from high school because a friend of mine had gotten it. All I remembered was that she wound up going for lots of blood tests over and over again.

Lyme disease is an infection from a tick bite, Hartley. Usually, the tick gets to the human by traveling on deer, then onto plants, trees, vegetation, or even your dog or outdoor cat.

My mind started racing when the doctor gave me the news.

Ticks? Deer? I lived in New York City. How in the heck did I get that?

Then I recalled that not-so-great weekend with the not-so-great boyfriend in the Hamptons. I didn't go into the woods, but they did have a dog that spent a lot of time outside, in and out of the brush. I also remembered that tiny rash I had seen on my leg after the trip, the one with the oddly specific border. Of course. That had been it.

The doctor had been wrong. We didn't catch it early. It had been brewing in my body for nine months.

I was told not to worry. Two weeks of antibiotics and I'd be better. She explained that Lyme was a weird little bacteria and that the medicine might make me feel sicker at first, as the bugs got angry when killed.

And so began a journey that lasted a lot longer than two weeks. Try more like two years.

The antibiotics didn't really work for me. I took them for two weeks, then even opted to take them for a longer period at the suggestion of another doctor. The medicine did nothing but give me stomachaches.

In the meantime, the symptoms were wild. And I mean WILD. Sudden heart palpitations with no obvious trigger. The right side of my face around my eye looked normal but felt frozen half the time. Muscle weakness and random tingling in my fingers and toes. Vertigo where the whole room would suddenly spin. Or I'd feel like I was walking on slanted ground when it was actually perfectly flat concrete. (I pride myself on good balance, as you know, so this drove me mad.)

I'd also get some brain fog, which made focusing difficult.

That was fun on live television.

One afternoon, I was co-hosting a television show when, suddenly, as I was reading the teleprompter, the whole scene around it started spinning. I got through it and didn't fudge the words, but I have no idea how.

Another time, I was co-hosting while holding on to the couch for dear life because I felt like I was leaning over the edge of a Tilt-a-Whirl ride at an amusement park.

I went to four more doctors, including a neurologist and two homeopaths. They had very few answers. The medical consultations cost me a fortune. This was money I didn't have to spend. I didn't know what to do.

I kept it all to myself at work. I couldn't tell anyone on the set what was happening. I was worried they'd think I was making it up, or worse, that they'd believe me and think I was a liability. Sometimes I would call Grandma pre-show to help calm me down. She tried, but it was tough.

Unfortunately, these unsettling episodes occurred again. And again. I knew I had to fix my body. I went to a Chinese herbalist who gave me, you guessed it, herbs. They helped a little, but a couple of months later, I was still struggling.

Coincidentally, I finally found help close to the scene of the crime, when I met a holistic, integrative doctor on Long Island. He took the time to listen to me about what I was feeling. We talked about my body, my mind, my emotions, and the connections between them. He helped me to detox my body and my mind. His supplements were healing. I was already a healthy eater, but he asked me to take it up a notch for the next six weeks. He insisted on solid sleep, eight hours a night, and doing what I could to keep stress at bay. This was a time for healing, and all of the elements of my body would need to work together and support one another.

I was on board. I dove right in.

I did a deep food cleanse and followed the supplement protocol to a T. Just weeks into it, I was feeling better. No fog, no vertigo. Weeks later, it continued to get better and better.

A solution without prescription drugs. It was possible and it was happening.

I monitored my exercise, getting just enough, but not doing too much. I alternated between meditative stretches, weight lifting, and cardio. I was in touch with my emotions and began to better understand how anger and stress affected me. I read a lot of books and dug into the research on nutrition even more. I became aware of the products in our home—the cleaning products, furniture, and other elements that could release toxins. I started to make better choices. I recognized that what I put onto my skin, the largest organ of the body, would be absorbed into my body. I did an entire makeover of my makeup and skin-care regimen.

I also realized that, of course, no one can avoid all of the toxins around them. That's not a realistic goal for any of us. But I wanted to minimize my exposure to them as best I could, to make things as easy as possible for my body to recover.

I got better.

I remain better.

Even when COVID-19 struck my body, I came out okay. I zeroed in on the lessons I had learned from my Lyme journey and let them guide me toward wellness.

I'm not grateful for contracting Lyme disease, Hartley. If I could go back in time and not go to the Hamptons that weekend, I would. For many reasons.

I am grateful, though, for what I learned from my recovery. It gave me a deeper appreciation for the interconnectedness of good health, good food, sleep, and a positive mindset.

Good health also gave me some superpowers. I learned that the healthier you make your body, the more sensitive it becomes to every-day poisons. I can smell bad chemicals in paint three houses down the street. A guest comes into our home with a toxic, allergenic perfume and my nose perks up right away. When we moved to Staten Island last year, my eyes suddenly started to itch like crazy. I knew there was something wrong in the house. Everyone thought I had lost it, but sure enough, the experts came in for an inspection and discovered there was a massive mold problem underneath the house.

I'm a pretty solid toxin-detector these days.

I'd love for you to have those superpowers without going through the bad stuff I had to go through to get them. I'd love for you to care deeply about your health and get your mind and body into a beautiful place where they speak to each other. I'm hoping to share lots of tools with you about how you can arm your body to help protect itself against invaders.

Our current home, Hartley, is our temple. We use nontoxic cleaners and nontoxic paints, and you play with nontoxic baby toys. I even bought you some veggie chalk and beeswax crayons. I'm telling you, I don't mess around. All of your play mats, your gated baby room, and your little sofa are free of nasty chemicals. I pay special attention to toys you might put in your mouth. We buy organic bedding from companies I know and love, whose materials are sourced in good, transparent places. Our dog, Daisy, even has plant-based shampoo and toothpaste.

We make everything you eat. It's a lot of work, and don't think there aren't times I just want to reach for the box, but I'm determined to give you the passion and purpose we have for a healthy body. We've got quite the menu going on. You have an organic fruit and veggie smoothie every day for one of your snacks. So far, you love them. I mix in some coconut water and different fruits each day, along with either spinach leaves or other greens. The combination of blueberry-banana-strawberry-spinach is your current favorite. I also make one for myself, with some different ingredients. I'll sometimes sub my favorite almond milk for the coconut water and add some spirulina and barley grass juice powders. I mix up the flavors for us every day, and Daddy has one, too, of whatever we make. It's a good way to get those fruits and veggies in. I also share with you my very special dessert smoothie—made with bananas, almond butter, dates, pistachio milk, and unsweetened cocoa—that tastes like chocolate milk, only better.

Your favorite homemade foods are sweet potato wedges and banana-oat pancakes. You also love celery juice and almond butter on bananas. You're not big on meat yet, but I do offer you organic chicken from a local farm we love, which you sample here and there. Same goes for organic, grass-fed steak and wild salmon. My wish is to have almost all of your food be homemade. I even bake you homemade cookies with freshly ground almond butter, oats, dark chocolate chips, and pure maple syrup for special occasions, and you are wild for them.

Daddy and I follow the same pattern of homemade goodies. Big salads, fresh soups, lots of fruits and veggies, high-quality meats and fish here and there. That's what makes the Bila-Scher house run.

All of this home cooking can be very time-consuming (and sometimes frustrating for someone like me who is definitely not a pro in the kitchen). But the way our bodies feel makes it worth it to us. Even Daisy gets a mix of homemade meats and an organic food I found through a holistic vet. I even went to meet the guy who owns the brand.

I think you get the picture that I take this food stuff seriously.

I hear people say sometimes that they can't afford to do all of this, that they don't have the money, let alone the time. I hear and understand all of those feelings. I share with them that when I first made big dietary changes, back in my acid reflux days, I did so on a teacher's salary. I cut back everywhere I could to make healthy food a priority. Holistic doctor visits can cost more, to be fair, but if you're ever in a situation where you're scared for your health, nothing will be as important to you as getting to the bottom of what's wrong. Taking ownership of your health, and reaping the physical and mental rewards of your good choices, is worth the extra time and money now. Think of the alternative: more trips to doctors, not feeling well enough to go to work or climb professional ladders, more payments and co-payments on prescriptions. I've found that in the long run, an emphasis on healthy, quality food and products pays off when it comes to your body and your wallet.

I hope you'll think about what goes into your body and how it makes you feel. I'm not saying there aren't going to be times you will want to eat junk, Hartley. And you will eat it, no doubt. Life is full of cake at birthday parties, holiday goodies at family gatherings, pizza at school, and hanging out at the diner after a movie with friends. I want you to experience all of those things, enjoy them, and not think twice about sharing a chocolate milkshake on your first date. (Yes, Mama's a little retro.) But I'm hopeful that your baseline will be good nutrition, with detours into junk food the exception, not the rule. Most importantly, I hope that you'll know your body well enough to feel the difference when you eat this versus that, and to care about that difference.

I also want to cook and bake *with* you, to learn together.

I try to think of food as a fun exploration of things that taste good and can help you feel good. Knowing that I have some control over my health when it comes to food has been powerful for me. It may be powerful for you too.

You will ultimately grow into an adult who makes these decisions for yourself. It will be up to you to choose how you want to eat and what your relationship with food will be like. I'll try to guide you the best I can, knowing that if you ever face a health obstacle of any kind, I want you to be in the best possible body to face it.

Also, I hope you're a way better cook than I am. That would be a win for us all.

I love you more than life,
Mama

No to Yes

Dear Hartley,

When I first started working in television, I got advice from a colleague who was more seasoned than I was at the time. She told me, "Say yes to everything." By that, she meant to appear everywhere I was invited, to always be ready to talk on-air about whatever a show producer wanted me to talk about, to get as much exposure as possible, and to not pass up an opportunity to be seen and heard.

Because she was more experienced than I was, I took her advice.

And now I'm telling you not to.

Say no, Hartley. When it comes to a career, say no to paths you don't want to pursue. Say no to opportunities that don't feel right or ones you don't like.

When I got that "Say yes to everything" television advice, it resonated because I had, unfortunately, been a yes-person my whole life. If you wanted me to be somewhere at a certain time, I was there. If you needed something? Yes, I would do it. I couldn't really understand how a person could be any other way. Was there any other choice? Someone asked you to do something, you did it.

And so, I started my television career and said yes to everyone and everything.

A segment on this morning show on this topic? Yes. In.

A panel on that afternoon show on that topic? Yes. In.

I said yes regardless of content, whether it was an area I wanted to discuss or not, whether it was paving the way for a career trajectory I wanted to be on or not.

I soon realized that if I agreed to discuss certain content and did okay at it, I'd likely be asked back to talk about similar content again. But what if I hated the content? What had I gotten myself into?

Basically, I made a lot of bad decisions that put me in places and spaces where I didn't belong, talking about things I didn't want to talk about. I know the cliché: Say yes to everything, you never know where it could lead. But in my case, it was leading me where I didn't want to go.

Think about the big picture of your life when you make these decisions that seem small at the time, but certainly add up. You have the power to make your path go this way or that way, or another way entirely. You may be offered jobs that have plenty of perks, jobs that others would kill for. But you're not others. You're you. Check in with yourself and make sure it's a job you actually want.

Sometimes, by saying no, you will lose an opportunity. But it's not a loss if it's an opportunity you didn't want.

If you see an open door, consider it, be grateful for it, and decide if you want to walk through it. If you don't, move on. Sure, that may shut some other doors down the road, but again, it's a pathway you don't want. Remind yourself of that.

In the same way, if you see another door out there that's right for you and it's closed, keep knocking. Knock hard. And often.

It's tricky, I know, but only you can make these choices. Only you will know which ones are the right ones and which ones are the wrong ones. If you're anything like me, you'll make a lot of mistakes along the way. You'll say yes when you should have said no, and no when you should have said yes. But you can always pivot. You can always change your mind. And just because you closed one door way back when doesn't mean there isn't another door out there that could also lead you to the place you want to be.

Follow your gut.

And if you have to slam a couple of doors along the way to stand up for yourself, slam away.

I love you more than life,
Mama

Desert Island Dude

Dear Hartley,

Picture this. The plane has crashed. Everyone survived. But there you are, stranded on a desert island. There are doctors, lawyers, musicians, teachers, and real estate brokers on board, but you are the only one who knows how to cut palm branches to build a hut or how to fashion tools for catching food. Cool, right? I mean, think about it—how great would it be if you were the guy everyone wanted to be stranded with on a desert island?

Super cool, indeed. Because that would mean you had practical, tangible skills. And having those skills has to be one of the best feelings ever.

The world in 2021 has become one of convenience, access, and full-service support. We don't need to know how to do anything anymore, it seems. We eat food we don't hunt or gather, we wear clothes we don't make, and we live in houses we don't build.

You get the picture. The problem is that important skill sets have been lost. I can't help but consider what the long-term impact of that will be.

Unfortunately, Daddy and I aren't the best role models in this area, though Daddy is significantly better than I am. Something happened just today, in our house, that prompted me to write you this letter.

Our water was brown. Everywhere. The bathroom, the kitchen, the shower. Your daddy called the plumber, who explained that there had been some work done in the back of the condos where we live, which was causing the water to turn brown, and that we needed to run the water outside for about forty-five minutes to get it back to normal. So I went out to the front lawn and ran the hose. After ten minutes or so of standing out there, hose in hand, one of our neighbors approached and asked what I was doing. I explained about our water. The kind gentleman suggested that perhaps the plumber meant we needed to run the hose in the back of our condo, where the work had been done, to flush out the right pipes. I laughed. Daddy also laughed when I told him the story minutes later.

"We need to learn stuff," he said.

I used to joke to your daddy as we watched *The Walking Dead* that if a horde of zombies came around, we'd probably be eaten first. Survival skills aren't our strong suit. Your mama is the kind of gal who would last about a minute and a half on *Survivor* or *Naked and Afraid*, two reality shows that test your survival skills when stranded in the great outdoors.

Daddy and I have a friend who lives on a self-sufficient, full-service farm he and his family run. He also homeschools his little girl. Part of her education is to care for the animals and grow her own food. That kid is ten years old and has better survival skills than I do. Our farmer friend handles his own plumbing, carpentry, even tackles glitches in the electrical wiring. He has storages of food and supplies in case of emergencies. I sometimes feel like he lives in an alternate universe. There he is, operating all of that stuff on his own, and I'm over here trying to screw in a lightbulb properly.

Hartley, I really want you to learn practical skills. Metalwork, woodworking, auto shop, candlemaking, tailoring—any of it would be good. It would be wonderful if you were the guy people called when they needed to put up shelving, build a loft, wire a lamp, fix a toilet, stitch a new jacket, or seal a driveway. Imagine the sense of reward that must come with being able to take care of your home and the homes of others that way.

When you can do practical things, you come to feel that if worse comes to worst, you can build or fix what's necessary to keep living, to keep thriving.

We saw this during the pandemic as the city shut down and we could no longer rely on the infrastructure and support services of a thriving metropolis. When things broke inside our home during that time, they often stayed broken for a while. It would have been great if we could've relied on ourselves to fix them, rather than others.

Self-sufficiency is such an admirable trait. Yet, how many of us who value it are in fact really self-sufficient?

The problem is that practical skills aren't taught in many schools. Unless you're lucky enough to have parents with hard-core skills like the ones we've been talking about, you're really on your own to learn those things. Living in apartment buildings for decades, where the super and handymen are available at all hours of the day and night, doesn't help either. It makes you lazy about certain things, less inclined to figure them out on your own. That's not an excuse, but it's the way it goes down sometimes.

One time, a huge storm was headed toward the city. I was advised by a friend to make sure the batteries in my flashlight were fresh.

"My what?"

"Your . . . wait a minute. You don't have a flashlight?"

"No."

"You need supplies for a storm, J."

He was right, though I knew that if I had supplies, I wouldn't know what to do with most of them anyway. Regardless, I listened to my friend and bought them.

I can cook decently, but nothing too complicated. I made chicken breasts the other night and sent a photo to your Uncle Mikey.

"What is that?" he asked.

"Chicken breasts."

"They look like burnt sweet potatoes. What did you do to them?"

I even started posting some food videos on Instagram, but with the hashtag #BadChefBila. Very, very fitting.

I put a chair together once, the only thing I've ever assembled in my life. I was darn proud of myself too. I remember being on the phone with a friend and the next thing I knew, I was on the floor. The chair had collapsed beneath me. My handiwork at work.

It makes me sad that I'm not good at fixing things. So I'm trying hard these days to do better, especially since you were born. When people come to the house to do repairs, I listen to what they're saying and doing. Daddy, in particular, is on a mission to learn from the plumbers and carpenters who come to our home. He wants this badly because he wants to be able to teach it to you one day.

It's baby steps, but steps nonetheless. I can even hang pictures with those stick-on Velcro strips. Sure, I pull paint off the wall whenever I remove them. But at least I can hang the stuff, right?

Baby steps.

I'm hoping that by the time you're a little bigger, Daddy and I will be better at all of this stuff and can teach you a few things.

Hopefully, one day, you'll teach us some things too. I can't believe I went through twenty-two years of schooling and didn't learn how to actually *do* anything. Fancy degrees don't always prepare you for the day-to-day challenges of life.

When I was pregnant with you, I watched the movie *The Notebook* for the five hundredth time. In that story, the main character, a rough-around-the-edges, blue-collar worker, rebuilds an old abandoned house that his one-time girlfriend fell in love with. They had once wandered around inside it, and she shared all of her hopes for the place. They were forced to go their separate ways for a while due to her family's disapproval and actions taken to keep them apart, but he bought and worked on that house she loved, building her dream home, hoping that one day it would bring her back to him. When they reunite years later, she goes to visit him and sees the house, just as she had imagined it, rebuilt by him from the ground up.

I've watched that film character tear down and rebuild that house so many times. Every time, I think the same thing: I'd rather have that skill set than my master's degree. I'm in complete awe of skills like that. Buying a house built by someone else just isn't the same.

I remember thinking, while watching that movie and rubbing my belly with you inside it, how I'd love to have a child who could build something. It doesn't have to be a house. It could be a toy chest, a desk, even a doghouse for our little Daisy.

I wish for you the feeling of self-reliance that must come from being able to build and fix the things we need and cherish.

I wish for you the sense of empowerment that must come from feeling able.

I will do everything I can to get you closer to people who will teach you these things. Daddy and I are doing our best to learn too.

And if you're lucky enough to be in a school that offers wood-working, I hope you'll take it. If I could go back in time, I'd trade in my AP Calculus for woodworking any day of the week.

I love you more than life,
Mama

Mama Lives Hungry

Dear Hartley,

A magical, illuminated castle stood tall and bright against the still-dark morning sky. I stopped and stared at it for a few moments. Wow.

It was as if I had been dropped right into a fairy tale. Which I had, because I was in Disney World. And it was Cinderella's castle I was mesmerized by in that moment.

I wasn't just *in* Disney World. I was in Disney World before the park had even opened, before the sun had even risen, to film some fun segments for *The View*. My co-hosts Sunny and Sara had been sent there with me to tape a montage that would air when we returned a month later to do a week of live shows from Animal Kingdom.

I had been to Disney before with Grandma and Grandpa when I was a kid, but seeing the castle lit against the sky while the park was still closed, with so few people around us, felt surreal. A good surreal. The kind of surreal you feel when you know you've stumbled upon a wonderful piece of your journey that you will treasure forever.

And I surely do.

I love Disney World. Well, any theme park really, but especially Disney. It's the ultimate in amusement parks because not only is it fun, but all of the rides and the sites you see are so beautiful. There's something incredible about the way Disney brings fairy tales to life. Being there helps you forget about your worries and stressors for a little while, helps you remember what it was like to be a wide-eyed, energetic kid seeing spectacular things for the very first time. Plus, your mama's the roller-coaster queen, which you'll come to know all too well.

That February weekend filming with Sunny and Sara was beyond hilarious. Sunny hates roller coasters and scary rides, so of course we filmed her going on all of them with us. The footage was perfection. The three of us laughed a lot. We got very little sleep and did tons of walking, so we were tired, but it was a good tired from having too much fun all day long. I remember the first afternoon we filmed in the Magic Kingdom.

"Where's Jed?" I heard Sunny ask Sara.

They both turned to see me staring up at a ride with my mouth full.

"You want some?" I asked. I held out a big bag of dried mangoes.

Sara looked at Sunny, Sunny at Sara.

"How did she get that?" Sara said.

Sunny: "Are you eating again, Jed?"

And so began a running joke, that everywhere we went, I somehow managed to have a different snack to eat and share.

As you may have started to learn already, Hartley, Mama lives hungry. I'm pretty active, so I guess it makes some sense. I'm also a picky eater, though, with my love for healthy foods. And so, I'm kind of a traveling supermarket when I go anywhere. I always have snacks in my pocket, in my jacket, in my bag, somewhere. And water. You will always find me with snacks and water. Airplanes. Long car rides.

Short car rides. Long walks. Short walks. Twelve-hour treks through Disney. You can count on me for snacks and water through it all.

I've learned that a hungry Bila or a thirsty Bila isn't a happy Bila, so I come prepared.

When we returned to Disney a month later with the whole team, even more fun ensued. *The View* was really good about welcoming family into all parts of the show, so a lot of family members of the cast and crew joined us on the trip. Your daddy came along, and we ate our way through all of Disney's parks. I even found lots of on-site healthy options. You'd be surprised what you can find when you give a good look around.

Don't worry, Hartley, you'll get to Disney soon enough. Mama and Daddy will make sure of it. And when you get there, I will have your back with plenty of drinks and snacks to keep you hydrated and happy while we hit all the rides together.

Always remember that life throws us a lot of curveballs. Unexpected traffic on the freeway, a flat tire in the middle of nowhere, a very long line in a store that you didn't anticipate. I promise that you will be infinitely happier every single time if you pack a snack. Or two. Or three. You get the picture.

I love you more than life,
Mama

We the People (Can Heal the Planet)

Dear Hartley,

My second apartment in Manhattan was one of my favorites. It was bigger than my first. I went from 375 square feet in my first apartment to around 550 square feet in my second. It felt like an enormous difference. I got really lucky with the second place because a friend of a friend owned the building. As a result, I had the chance to live in an alcove studio in a doorman building for a great price. I also liked the Midtown location, as I was on Fifty-Eighth Street and Lexington Avenue, just two subway stops from work.

I was thrilled on moving day. Grandma and Grandpa bought me a new couch for the space, and I spent the first few days organizing and getting settled. In many ways, that was the first time I felt all grown up. I finally had the New York City apartment I had dreamt of as a kid.

Everything was going great until one night around 6:00 p.m., a week or so after I moved in. I had been inside all day cleaning and working, but caught a glimpse of the weather report and figured it would be a great time to shut off the air conditioning and get some fresh air into my new space. I opened the largest of three windows. WHOA. That was *not* fresh air. All I got was a big whiff of car exhaust. I closed the window immediately and looked out. I was on the second floor, and when I looked down, I saw bumper-to-bumper traffic headed toward the Fifty-Ninth Street Bridge. Uh-oh. I had never even thought about that. I looked at the outside surface of my windows and they had a gray, dirty film on them. Yuck.

I started thinking.

Sure, the pollution outside my window was concentrated and right in my face because of traffic being so close, but the reality was that trucks, cars, taxis, trains, boats, and buses were pushing pollution into the Manhattan skyline daily. I was walking through it all the time, to and from work, to and from the grocery store, to and from the gym. That wasn't good.

I bought an air purifier for my apartment. I also almost never opened my windows, except on weekend afternoons when the traffic was way less congested. Keeping the windows closed most of the time was my only way to avoid that horrible smell of car exhaust.

Ever since then, I've thought a lot about the environment, our place in it, and how we can help make things better. I've researched how eco-friendly products also tend to be much healthier for us humans. I've switched over to green cleaning products for our home and green wellness products for our faces, hair, and bodies. I've traded plastic storage containers for glass and food-grade silicone ones. I even found plant-based straws that we love. Yep, you read that right.

I've tried to switch everything I can to reusable options that are safer for the environment and for us. I now have two air purifiers running in our home, which makes a really big difference in the indoor air quality. I filter the water we drink because I want us to have the cleanest drinking water possible, while also avoiding an accumulation of plastic bottles. It makes me sad, though, that our house has to have filters to guard against what would otherwise come through the air and water.

When I think about the environment, I want to be part of the solution. I want our family to be part of it. I want the solution to be driven by people—thoughtful, motivated people who care about their families and the world around them. The way I see it, the path to a healthier planet, healthier homes, and healthier families is through us, all of us. Knowledge about all of this stuff is key too. People can't be inspired to make changes unless they know how their health stands to benefit from it all. I plan to make it a priority to get that information out there.

We the people can improve our habits, make better choices, and reap the health benefits of those choices for years to come.

I don't know how you'll feel about the environment as you grow. As of today, you flock to the ocean, stare up at the sky, and love being in sunshine. But when it comes to any issue that you care about, be it the environment or something else, think about your capacity to make a difference in your own life and the lives of others. You have the incredible power of choice. You have the choice to arm yourself with knowledge, to share what you know, to buy certain products over others, and to invest your time, energy, and money in the things you believe in.

Never feel powerless.

And if you grow up and find yourself loving the trees and the ocean as much as you do today, do what you can to protect them. Remember, we're all connected in this universe—people, nature, everything.

I love you more than life,
Mama

Spring-Cleaning (Closet Cleaner)

Dear Hartley,

Everyone handles stress differently. Some people eat too much ice cream, others bite their nails down to nothing, and I...clean out closets.

What can I say? That's my thing. I'm a spring-cleaning closet cleaner.

Except that I don't just do it in the spring. And I don't just do it when I'm stressed. I clean out closets when I'm excited or nervous, when I'm waiting for an important phone call or waiting to give birth. When I was pregnant with you, I cleaned out every closet in the apartment three times. My friends would joke, "Oh, she's nesting." Nope, not nesting. I had cleaned out those closets three times the year before too.

When your daddy sees me coming with empty garbage bags, he knows where I'm headed.

"Those T-shirts aren't old!" he shouts as I giddily run upstairs, ready to embark on a closet-purging and reorganizing effort. He follows me up to supervise, knowing full well that the T-shirts in question *are* old and on their way out.

I clean out closets so often that I pretty much have no clothes left. This works out, though, because I'm an ever-increasing minimalist. When it comes to your closet, there's always lots to donate because you're growing so quickly that what fits you one month doesn't fit you the next. Donating clothes always puts a great big smile on my face. I place all of the old garments into bags and drop them off at shelters and clothing drives.

Grandma calls closet cleaning my healthy drug of choice. "You look so relaxed today. Did you clean out the closets?" she asks on the regular.

Yep.

I sure did.

I love the idea of parting with old garments. Out with the old, in with the new. Even when there's nothing new, out with the old feels pretty good too. I love the feeling of saying goodbye to clothes that don't fit right anymore, don't appeal to me anymore, or remind me of nights I don't want to remember. There's something oddly rejuvenating about it all. And then, an added bonus—the reorganizing I get to do once the items I've parted with are gone.

Of course, I save a few sentimental items. Like the outfit I took you home from the hospital in, a couple of special logo tees that Daddy and I bought each other, and that unitard I had the audacity to wear on Fifth Avenue in broad daylight when I was twenty-two. Some items hold too many fun memories to hit the trash or donation pile.

So the next time you see me in the early morning with my head in the closet while scarves, shoes, and belts fly out behind me, know that your mama is in the happiest of her happy places. And that none of us will likely have any clothes left by noon.

My wish for you is to find a wonderfully productive, healthy, and generous way to de-stress that makes you as happy as closet cleaning makes me.

And if you ever need help cleaning out closets anywhere, anytime, you know who to call.

I love you more than life,
Mama

Festive Fun

Dear Hartley,

One cold December afternoon just after Thanksgiving, a couple of months after I met your daddy, I took a walk down Fifth Avenue to clear my brain. It had been a particularly tough day at work, with fast and furious news cycles churning and political agendas burning.

I wanted to remind myself why I got into television in the first place. I knew what the answer was, and here comes this concept again—to create and be part of good conversations. Really good conversations that could get us all reflecting and learning about the world and one another. Life can be hard, struggles challenging, and I know that when we reached for the TV remote in my house growing up, it was often to try to lift us up in some way. Maybe we'd flip on a funny movie, a sitcom, or a great on-air conversation with topics we would carry over to our dinner table. I wanted to find that good television conversation again, wherever and however I could.

It didn't take long before I came upon Rockefeller Center and the big, beautifully lit tree that soared over the ice-skating rink. I remembered that when I was twenty-three, just a few days before Christmas, your Aunt Lauren and I rode the Zamboni over that rink and had a blast. I briefly dated a guy who managed Rock Center Café at the time, so Zamboni rides were a perk. Cutting the line to skate wasn't so bad either.

I also remembered what I always knew: getting into the spirit of the holidays really makes me feel good. Even though holidays bring a special kind of joy to us when we're little, we also downright cherish them as adults. A break from life's challenges, upsets, and busy schedules is a welcome gift for us all.

When I was a kid, we had a very festive house. Christmas meant a big Christmas tree full of ornaments, a giant wreath on the front door, garland down the stairs, and Grandma's perfectly wrapped presents under and around the tree. Grandma bought the best wrapping paper. She'd wrap each gift in paper that suited the person the gift was for, like paper with cats and dogs on it for me, and paper with baseballs and basketballs on it for Grandpa. Your Great-Aunt Joan used to bake the most delicious homemade chocolate chip cookies and send us giant Christmas tins with them inside. I'd wait for those tins to arrive every year. And our house always smelled so good around the holidays from all the homemade cooking, especially the lasagna.

One Christmas, Grandma, who is super artistic as you know, decided that instead of a traditional evergreen tree, she was going to assemble several large bamboo poles into a giant Christmas vase, wrap Christmas bows around the poles, and create a bamboo tree. At the time, I was like, *Mom, what in the heck are you doing?* But it worked. It was bizarre in the way that a lot of Grandma's creations are, in that the idea seems super weird at first, but somehow winds up looking gorgeous.

There's one "decoration" I almost forgot to mention—the holiday movies that were often playing in the background throughout the house. I know, I know, Christmas movies aren't technically a decoration. But in an unconventional, think-outside-the-box head—and house—they sure can be. Grandma used to have *The Bishop's Wife* with Cary Grant on a lot at Christmastime because she loves Cary Grant and loves angels, and that movie has both. *Grumpy Old Men* would crack us up each time we watched it as if we'd never seen it before. Movies were playing around us often, as we cooked delicious meals, enjoyed holiday treats next to the fireplace, or cuddled before bed.

We'd also drive around at Christmastime to see the neighbors' outdoor lights. There was this one house nearby that went all out—multicolored lights of all sizes, big candy canes, a moving Santa Claus cutout that was riding moving reindeer. It was amazing.

We'd drive around to see decorations during other holidays too.

There was a house just down the street that would decorate for Halloween with all sorts of ghosts and goblins on their lawn, fake spiderwebs, and other decorations to make it look like a real-life haunted house, which I loved. On Halloween night, the owners would even dress up in scary costumes to greet trick-or-treaters. We had some fun Halloween decorations at our house too—a big pumpkin filled with treats, a scarecrow, and some ghost cutouts on our little lawn. I'd dress up every year. One year, Grandma dressed up as a baby, diaper and rattle included. We had matching costumes. Grandma was fun like that.

At Easter, I'd get a basket filled with some of my favorite treats and toys, and we'd have an indoor or outdoor (depending on weather) Easter egg hunt to find colorful plastic eggs with goodies inside. Sometimes Grandpa would even put money inside that I could put in my piggy bank.

Thanksgiving was big in our house too. Course after course of homemade food and colorful baskets everywhere, filled with squash and pumpkins.

I shared all of those traditions with family, friends, and some of my parents' friends who felt just like family. One Christmas, Grandma had a big party in our little condo. I'll never figure out how we fit so many people into our living room. Two big tables full of guests, more food than I could describe, and lots of singing and dancing. One of Grandma's friends played guitar and sang, so we had live music right there in our living room.

Grandma would also lead a prayer at the dinner table at all holiday gatherings, thanking God, Jesus, and the Holy Spirit for the food and family that we were so lucky to have before us.

As an adult, when I lived on my own, I continued a lot of these traditions. For Easter, I would get a basket that I'd fill with homemade treats for Easter Sunday. I had a Christmas tree with ornaments every year. Sometimes the tree was small, especially in my studio apartments, but it was a tree nonetheless, and when it would light up the room at night, I always felt at peace. I'd even dress up and go to Halloween parties sometimes too.

I continued Grandma's tradition of prayer on Christmas, Easter, and Thanksgiving. I may have worded things a little differently than she did, making it my own, but I'd thank God, the universe, the sun, and the stars for the gifts of family, friends, and food that I was lucky enough to savor.

I also carried with me into adulthood a special Christmas ornament tradition. Ornaments have always been very important in our
family. Each one had, and still has, meaning. Your Great-Aunt Joan
used to send us fun ornaments every Christmas that would reflect
some aspect of our lives the prior year. For example, if I had learned
to swim that year, I got a pool ornament. Grandma and Grandpa
would buy ornaments on our vacations too. On our family tree
now, I have special ornaments for you, me, Daddy, and even Daisy.
I have an ornament given to me and Daddy by a dear friend at our
wedding, an ornament Daddy and I bought in Italy on our honey-
moon, ornaments featuring skis and pizza and all of the things
Daddy loves, and old-fashioned roller skates and memorabilia from
Friends and *90210* for me. There's a little chicken leg ornament for
Daisy (her favorite food), a baby rattle and avocado ornament for
you (your favorite food), and a photo ornament of our dog Emma,
who's now in puppy heaven.

The tree isn't just a tree. It's *us*. It represents all of us. Together.

As far as movies, Daddy and I have cuddled up on the couch
the last few Christmas seasons with some great films that kept us
laughing and thinking. *The Family Man* is a good one if you ever have
one of those *What if I had taken this path in life instead of that one* kind
of days. There are so many good holiday movies, and each of them
reminds us that it's a season for eating good food, spending time
with good people, and being grateful for the gifts around us that
don't come in boxes or gift bags.

Food was a big part of both your daddy's and my holiday celebrations growing up, and we have kept that tradition alive. In fact, the
food often feels as much a part of the decor as the decorations, and
we wouldn't have it any other way.

For now, you enjoy watching us decorate, participating here and there. You love unloading pre-holiday groceries, endless bags of goodies that cook up to even better goodies. You loved our Christmas tree this year. We had to elevate it on a wooden block because you and Daisy were a little too interested in tugging at the branches, but you'd smile so big when we'd turn on the lights. Soon enough, you'll help decorate the tree, pick out ornaments, and take your full part in all of these traditions. And one day, you'll come up with ideas for traditions of your own, which we'd love to incorporate and make part of our celebrations.

Decorating for the holidays makes a real difference, Hartley. It fills the house with hope and reminds us of our joy, past and present. It separates the holiday from the everyday.

I hope you'll always have some holiday decorations around you. I hope you make them special and unique to you, and that you let them light up your living room and your life. I hope you know the feeling of looking at Christmas tree lights when the rest of the room is dark. It's pretty amazing. When the years get busy, or you have to travel for work, or life gives you one of those seasons filled with rough spots, remember that holiday decorations and holiday cooking can make all the difference in shifting your thinking and warming your soul.

I hope that you and your generation hold on to holidays. I hope that you don't become so immersed in the virtual world that you forget how much fun it is to hang stockings and carve pumpkins.

Life is strange sometimes, Hartley. You get caught up, you forget who you are, you lose your focus. If you're lucky, you find your way back to yourself and the things that matter to you pretty quickly. I know it sounds silly now, but holiday decorations always brought out the best in me—the laughter, the lightheartedness, the love. And in doing so, they always helped me navigate back to a path that felt right. Maybe, just maybe, they'll do the same for you.

I love you more than life,
Mama

Time Out from Tech

Dear Hartley,

Grandma came into our house the other day and said, "It's so quiet in here." You were in the corner of your play gym busily flipping through the pages of one of your favorite books. The television was off. Mommy and Daddy's cell phones were plugged into a nearby charging station that we would sometimes visit, mostly to check in with work. Daddy was cooking and I was watering some indoor plants while listening to the faint sound of chirping birds through an open kitchen window.

Grandma was right.

It was quiet.

Daddy and I have tried our best to leave room for those quiet times without television or computer background noises. Of course, you make plenty of fun noises all on your own, and some not-so-fun ones, like when we have to change your diaper and you're less than happy about it. You laugh a lot, thankfully, and that adorable laughter carries through the whole house. I love that sound so much.

It's the tech sounds that we don't like droning on and on within our walls—no constant television background noise, no wild and crazy baby toys that make loud sounds on repeat, no nonstop music playing.

When Daddy and I want to watch a TV show at night after you've gone to bed, we turn on the television, watch it, then turn it off when the show is done.

We even give you some time each day to dance along with your favorite television buddies, the *Bubble Guppies*. But after a little bit, the TV goes off and you go back to reading, climbing, or exploring. Or you head outside with us to the playground.

When we want to hear music, we listen for a while, dance, and sing. When we're done, we shut it off.

When we embrace the technology in our lives, it's intermittent, broken up by plenty of tech-free peace.

We also do one thing at a time.

When we read, that's what we're doing—reading. When we go out in the stroller, we talk. I'm not on my phone or listening to a podcast in those moments—I'm with you, listening for the opportunity to connect.

After a stage in his teenage years of video-game addiction, your daddy is a particularly low-tech guy. No social media. Almost no texting. Very little email. If he wants to connect with someone, he picks up the phone and calls them. He sets a great example for you.

A few years ago, before you were born, I wrote a book about the power of people to maintain their health, sanity, and positive relationships despite all of the technology we tend to drown in daily. I'm talking about emails, texts, social media, video games, apps, you name it. In that book, *#DoNotDisturb*, I shared deeply personal stories and tips to balance, not eliminate, the tech in our lives. I included plenty of mistakes I made with technology along the way. I even dug into the ways Silicon Valley is manipulating us like puppets, what we can do about it, and the positive and negative impacts of technology on all of us.

I love my technology as much as the next person. It's amazing to be able to text anyone, anywhere, and have them write you back so quickly. During the COVID-19 pandemic, the wonders of technology became highly visible and highly valuable. We could stream movies and television shows into our homes, order food from anywhere around town with the push of a button, and gather family and friends in little Brady Bunch squares on our computers for real-time gatherings. All without taking off our pajamas. Fitness companies and trainers adapted by creating fitness apps online. Some companies created and sold bikes and other equipment that would plug you into virtual fitness classes and virtual personal training sessions. Schools began computer-based remote learning programs. For many companies, our ability to be plugged into one another without being anywhere near one another suddenly became essential. Technology made all of that possible.

Of course, all of those things cost money as well, and the need for technology during the pandemic highlighted, and often magnified, the disadvantages faced by those with economic challenges. It made us think long and hard about economic discrepancies and how they impact quality of life, particularly in times of uncharted crisis.

Technology can bring about immense benefits, but not everything that comes from a tech boom is good. Cell phone addiction is very real, complete with an obsessive need to check in with social media, texts, and emails on a constant basis. An addiction like that takes a big toll on your health. There are even detox programs and retreats that exist to help combat that addiction. Some people live more in the world of technology than they do in the real one. In fact, there are computer games that allow people to create virtual versions of themselves and live entire virtual lives in virtual universes, coming back to the real world only to sleep and eat. Imagine how much real-life sunshine and how many real-life interactions they miss out on.

As you go through life with a ton of technology around you, remember your power to choose, to embrace what feels healthy and to reject what doesn't. Heaven only knows what apps will exist by the time you're a teenager. And sure, Silicon Valley will likely still program those apps to try to get us addicted. But again, you're way more powerful than those apps. You're a thinking, breathing human. You have the choice to pick up a phone or put it down, to download an app or delete it, to take the bait of addiction or instead use those devices in ways that enhance your life, but don't run your life.

It's the way Daddy and I use them now.

I hope that you and your generation won't allow your cell phone, or whatever device plugs you into everyone and everything by the time you're older, to become an appendage. I hope devices won't get in the way of in-person conversations across a dinner table, that they won't replace important in-person moments with impersonal texts or emails.

I hope that your generation wants to undo bad tech habits that have overtaken so much of life.

You're going to have to decide how you want to communicate with people, how engaged you want to be. My hope is that when you're on a date one day, that person will feel your focus, not see you distracted by a device or the people beckoning you from it. That focus, that attention, makes a world of difference to the person you're with. It affects how they feel about you and how they think you feel about them.

I'll play a big role in all of this, too, as you grow. As will other parents with their children. I hope that Daddy and I can help you navigate your way through old and new technologies, through the best ways to use devices and not let them use you. The onslaught of new phones and apps came so quickly over the last couple of decades that many of us got taken by surprise. The innovations were so exciting that we didn't have a chance, or make the time and effort, to take a long pause and consider the consequences of leaping into it all right away.

Take that pause, Hartley. Take it before embracing the next supposedly amazing tech distraction. Think about what that device or software might do to your life, to your relationships with others, to your relationship with yourself. Move slowly to embrace the things around you that pop up quickly.

And if you're ever engaged with your phone in a way that makes you forget about the person sitting in front of you, or even the trees and the sun and the sky around you, check in with yourself in that moment.

So many of us are here or there and everywhere, but so few are present.

Be present.

I love you more than life,
Mama

Emma

Dear Hartley,

I remember the day I got my first dog, Emma. She was so tiny, this little two-pound ball of white fur. Uncle Mikey, who was my roommate at the time, drove us to Upstate New York to see her at a farm that another friend was familiar with. That first day we met her, she crawled into Uncle Mikey's neck and I knew there was no way he was leaving without her. She looked up at me with big brown eyes while she cuddled on his shoulder. She was the most adorable dog I had ever seen.

Uncle Mikey and I co-parented Emma for eleven amazing years. When we were no longer roommates, she would spend weekdays with him (he'd take her to work a lot) and weekends with me. She loved your daddy, too, and would nap with him on Saturdays and take walks with him on sunny afternoons.

Sadly, Emma died of a heart attack when you were just seven months old. It was sudden and it broke my heart on many levels, including that you didn't get to know her better. You won't remember this, but she used to put her paws on my belly when you were in there and you'd kick back. You would also try to pull her tail when you were really small, and she would stomp her little feet to let you know she wasn't happy. She was feisty, just like you, right from the start.

Throughout her life, I was definitely Emma's second favorite (and a distant second) to Uncle Mikey, but I was okay with that because he was such a great parent to her. Uncle Mikey has the amazing gift of relating to animals in a way that most people can't. It's almost like he speaks dog and cat. Animals flock to him in parks, elevators, everywhere. I've seen them leave their owners' sides to be by his. It's remarkable.

Emma may have loved Uncle Mikey best, but she totally had my personality. She was stubborn and pretty antisocial. She loved home-cooked veggies and was hesitant to trust other dogs. She liked her circle small, but when she loved someone, she loved them like crazy.

I had a lot to learn about raising a dog when I got Emma. I got her when I was still teaching in Manhattan, and I remember how cuddling with her soothed my stress as I made big decisions about career changes, relationships, moves, and so much more. She would look up at me and reassure me that no matter what, it would all be okay. And it was.

Emma was me in a dog in so many ways. We just kind of understood each other. And that made all the difference at a time in my life filled with so many changes and so much uncertainty.

Hartley, a pet can be such a great companion. Someone to love with all your heart, someone who loves you back unconditionally and provides peace and loyalty when the world seems scary and lonely.

I hope that the world is never too scary and that you're never lonely. But I know that there will be those times. And if you have a pet like Emma, or like our current dog, Daisy, you will find that you have a piece of your heart to hug every day.

Let those furry little creatures teach you what they know. You'd be surprised how many keys they hold to life's unanswered questions. And when they leave us one day for pet heaven, know that they hover above us like little angels and we feel their presence when we need it most.

I love you more than life,
Mama

Descubrimientos

Dear Hartley,

Learning a second language was such a wonderful experience for me. It opened my mind and my heart.

At first, when I began my second-language learning in middle school and high school, I was doing it to fulfill the school's curriculum. I knew nothing about the exciting world about to open up for me.

In middle school, the curriculum included some basic Spanish classes, very basic. In high school, we had a language requirement, so I took Spanish because I felt like I had a head start from middle school. Plus, my mom's dear friend from Puerto Rico, Rose, spoke some Spanish around me growing up, so Spanish was a little familiar. One of my first words was "Mira!" because Aunt Ro Ro was always saying it and pointing here and there for me to look at this and that.

The Spanish I took in high school was mostly grammar. Grammar was my thing, so I did well. In college, I took my first couple of Spanish classes, Intermediate Spanish 1 and 2, because I figured they'd be guaranteed good grades. I was right. But I had this really great teacher who spoke five languages like they were all her native tongue. She spoke Spanish, English, Italian, French, and Portuguese, all fluently. That was intriguing to me. I was also intrigued when I saw her reading a novel in Spanish one day while we took a test. *Hmm, I wonder if I could do that.* I couldn't yet, but the idea was now in my mind. I decided to take the next two classes in the language series, Conversation and Composition 1 and 2. I did well in those, too, and was soon able to read short stories and short essays. It was so strange and wonderful how at some point, my mind stopped translating step-by-step while reading, and instead just read. I liked the feeling. So I moved on to Introduction to Literary Texts.

I was enjoying these language classes, so I just kept taking them. I remember reading my first full novel and writing my first full paper in Spanish, feeling like I had accomplished something major. I loved the whole vibe of the classes, the language, the literature, the culture, all of it. I even dated a guy in college who was a native Spanish speaker. I hadn't done so on purpose, but it did always seem like I was drawn to the language in one form or another.

Because I hadn't spent much time (translation: any time) in high school figuring out what I might want to do career-wise, I entered college pretty directionless. I thought about a psychology major, but wasn't sure I was mentally designed to help people in that way. I worried that my empathy would get the best of me and I'd never be able to lift people's worries off my shoulders at the end of a workday. I continued accruing credits in Spanish simply because I liked what I was studying. Then one day, I figured I would make Spanish my major.

"What in the heck will you do with that?" I was asked. A lot.

My plan was to teach it at the college level, but studying Spanish also just made me happy, so I went with it. Plus, I was doing well, which satisfied my need-for-great-grades obsession.

I remember the first time I read a menu in Spanish at a restaurant I had been to years before. Somehow it made the food taste even better. I also recall the first time I had a dream in Spanish. It was surreal in all the best ways.

It was when I started my PhD program at Columbia University that things changed. I was at the uppermost academic levels of speaking, reading, and writing, but my experience there wasn't good. The classes didn't have the warmth of my college classes, which had felt more like living room conversations. My teachers were smart, but not terribly friendly. There was little attention to cultural components. It didn't tap into what I had loved about studying Spanish and instead made me feel out of place.

I loved Spanish so much, but I wanted to indulge in the culture, enjoy the food, dance to the music. I wanted to learn from people who were warm and fun. I wanted to talk with teachers who were invested in the texts they chose for us and would share why those books meant so much to them.

I came to realize that my love of Spanish hadn't been about an academic pursuit, but rather a journey of self-discovery. Spanish opened the portal for me to learn more about myself. It taught me how to enjoy something for the sake of just enjoying it. It helped me to open my mind and my heart. I knew that the only way to preserve my love of Spanish was to leave Columbia behind and take the language with me.

I even got into teaching Spanish at different levels over the next decade to be certain that the academic angle wasn't for me. My initial instinct that it hadn't been the right career path proved correct. I ultimately moved on with a greater sense of purpose toward what felt right.

Learning another language can be an incredible experience, Hartley.

I'm hopeful you'll give it a try with any language you like. You may not take to it, but if you do, it can be pretty exciting. The ability to communicate with people in a different language brings a part of you alive that you otherwise may have never known existed.

I have this view that our bodies, our souls, our minds, and our hearts are each composed of different tiny parts, only some of which we can access. Languages poke their way into some of those seemingly inaccessible parts, making your skin tingle, your soul smile, your mind light up, and your heart beat a little faster.

When you fall in love for the first time, Hartley, you'll feel alive in a way that's very different than you've ever felt before. Learning languages sparks a similar awakening.

Spanish often slips into our conversations at home, so you've heard a lot of it by now. You love dancing to Latin music. I was trying to get you to dance the last time your Uncle Mikey visited, flipping through song after song and playing them. You weren't having it. Finally, I hit on a salsa song, and you dove right in.

"He's definitely your kid," Uncle Mikey said. And we laughed.

Maybe you'll pick up some words or phrases from me, maybe you won't. Maybe you'll love Spanish, maybe you won't. Maybe you'll fall in love with French, Italian, or Japanese and teach Mama and Daddy some things.

Spanish created a path for me to open up, to live life more deeply, and to trust my instincts. Keep your eyes open for the things in life that can do that for you.

Te quiero más que la vida,
Mama

Heartbreak & Healing

Dear Hartley,

Broken hearts are real and awful and happen to a lot of us. My mamabear instinct will want to protect you from ever getting one, but I know that I can't protect you from everything. I also know that there are a lot of lessons that come with overcoming a broken heart.

Your daddy was my first, and only, true love. I know that's hard to believe because I didn't meet him until my mid-thirties, but it's true. He is my soul mate, the first person I was ever able to envision sharing the rest of my life with.

That doesn't mean I didn't *think* I had met a true love before. Once, actually, a long time ago. Of course, my big, beautiful love for your daddy now puts that old relationship in proper perspective. At that time, though, way back when, I didn't yet know the kind of powerful love I would know with your dad, and why it would be so different from anything else I had felt before.

The relationship I'm referencing from long ago, when I was in my late teens, was tough. Not all of it, but too much of it. There were big lessons. One of those lessons involved heartache, heartbreak, how you recover from it all, and why recovering from it without building up walls to protect yourself is so important.

Hartley, broken hearts can feel pretty bad, kind of like your insides are sinking into your body and you can't pull them back out. Sometimes you miss someone, or think you do, and can't even articulate why. Sometimes you hold on to people because they're familiar and the familiarity seems safe, even when it's not. Sometimes letting people go feels impossible even when you really want to let them go. It all gets pretty complicated.

If and when your heart gets broken, you have to figure out how to navigate through the sadness, overcome it, and plant your feet firmly on the other side. It's normal to be afraid to open yourself up to love after you've been hurt in a relationship, but if you shut down after a broken heart, or if you give up, or if you close yourself off to possibilities because it all feels too scary after all of that hurt, you may never find the person you're really meant to be with.

Let's backtrack a bit.

Your mama didn't have a serious boyfriend until she was nineteen years old. I was what you might call a late bloomer to love. I had always been so focused on schoolwork that I never had space in my mind for anything else. I met my first real boyfriend when I was a college sophomore. He was the first person I was attracted to in a big way. He was funny and smart. He was also older than I was, and I liked that he was into art, restaurants, and good conversations. We started dating and I fell for him. I fell hard.

We spent a lot of time together. He was the first real dinner date I'd ever been on. We even took a few trips together, and so he became the first romantic partner I had ever vacationed with. He also had a great group of guy friends who were super welcoming of me right from the start. I loved hanging out in his best friend's house in Brooklyn watching movies, or heading with the whole crew to a nearby concert in the park.

The relationship was fun and intense the first year and a half, but then it got difficult. He had an opportunity to go abroad to work for a year, and neither of us handled that separation very well, not to mention that we each handled it completely differently. I missed him a lot and wanted the lines of communication to be super open while we were far apart. He told me he missed me too, but shut down when he couldn't handle the distance between us. It was a mess. He visited twice and I went to visit him once. We even met for a week in Puerto Rico for a getaway. All of those visits got complicated. There was always this feeling of super closeness when we were together, then someone would hit an airport and *BAM!*, he would shut down, pull away, and it would feel like he was gone. Not just physically, but emotionally. He would become completely unreachable for days at a time. His emails would read formal and distant. It was all so abrupt for me, to go from those super close moments in person to feeling like I was communicating with an acquaintance days later. My heart hurt a lot. I often felt like the person I loved was just out of reach. By the third time we saw each other that year, I remember getting on the plane to come home and feeling tired. I had been afraid to get too close to him on that trip for fear that he'd shut down again when we parted. I didn't want to risk feeling sad. Now *I* was the one shutting down, guarding my heart.

At some point, and I can't remember exactly when, I gave up. I didn't break up with him or see anyone else, but my heart just kind of stopped feeling. And in the process, I stopped feeling for him. I did what I do best and focused on my studies. Little by little, I became more and more distant from him. It wasn't an active decision. I think my body, or maybe my heart, or maybe both, just needed to step back. In stepping back, I lost touch with my love for him. We still emailed, but I no longer pushed for closeness in our written interactions. I'd just write about what I was up to and share day-to-day activities. I remember that he asked once why I was being so formal with him, and I didn't have an answer. The tables had turned and he sensed it. I wasn't behaving differently to get a reaction out of him. I just felt numb. And worse, the numbness didn't bother me. It made me feel everything less, and after feeling so much struggle and sadness for months, feeling less was a welcome change.

He came to my graduation with a giant bouquet of flowers, ready to start again. It was too late. I didn't hate him, wasn't mad at him, but the part of me that had loved him wasn't there anymore. I couldn't access it. I also knew that whatever damage had been done that year between us wasn't going to be fixed. Even if I could somehow figure out how to love him like I did before, I would always see him as someone who could shut me out like that, and I couldn't handle that again.

It took me a long time to get over that first love, Hartley. Even though I'm the one who ended the relationship, I was still holding on to some things. I had loved the way it felt to be in love with him, loved the way it made me walk through life with a skip in my step. I was afraid I'd never feel that way about anyone again, but also afraid of what could happen if I did.

I soon developed some bad relationship habits. At first, for months and months, I didn't want to date anyone. I wasn't interested. I couldn't imagine opening myself up to another person.

When I finally started dating, I would go out with guys I didn't really like that much, or ones I had a great friend-vibe with but wasn't attracted to. You see, if I wasn't into them that much, I wouldn't fall for them, and my heart would never get broken. Of course, I didn't do any of this consciously and only realized the pattern in retrospect. I guess it was my way of inching toward the romance department without actually diving in.

I soon realized that I had an even bigger problem: I just wasn't into anyone. I was out and about a lot, meeting all kinds of different people in all kinds of different settings, and wasn't meeting anyone I was even slightly worried about falling for. My college boyfriend had been someone I didn't seek out. He kind of fell into my view. But we had been drawn to each other in an odd, movie-ish kind of way, at least for me. No one was coming remotely close to that.

At some point, I decided to stop thinking about it all so much. I lived my life and figured I'd let the universe do its thing. I dated a little, but not much. I got to a place where I was open to feeling love again. I didn't know if it would happen, but I was open.

And then I met your daddy. Daddy took me completely by surprise. We worked out at the same gym and had several conversations in that gym. He is younger than I am, and I had always dated older guys, so my first impression was: *This could be a fun friend to hang out with.* We also seemed to have a lot of common interests, so that was cool.

We decided to meet outside the gym for lunch. We had another great conversation. We went on long walks, had great talks. And we would laugh, Hartley. We would laugh so much, more than I had ever laughed before. I loved hanging out with him and would really look forward to those days.

Then, he surprised me.

He told me he had feelings for me and wanted to date, for real.

The truth is, we were already in that zone of fall-in-love moments. We flirted all the time, leaned on each other in front of sunsets, shared secrets we'd never shared with anyone else. Daddy was, and is, attentive, thoughtful, funny, and kind. He's smart in all the ways I'm not and has the most generous spirit. Something about him felt like home right from the start.

We fell in love. A love like I had never known.

That love would never have happened if I hadn't been open to letting someone into the deepest parts of my heart again.

While I hope that no one ever hurts you, odds are that someone will. That's unfortunately the way life works. Maybe you won't want to talk about it. Maybe you'll want to process it all by yourself. I hope not, because the talking really helps. My best friends helped me through that broken heart of mine decades ago, and I don't know what I would've done without their friendship.

I will always be here to listen, Hartley.

If someone does break your heart, try your best, in your own time, to find your way back to feeling open. Because a month, a year, or a decade later, you may meet someone who feels like they were sent from the universe. I know that sounds crazy, but it happens. I felt like your daddy showed up from the clouds or the sun or the stars. I'm typically slow to warm up to others, but with him, there was an ease to it all that was oddly wonderful.

I'm so glad I was open. Because now I have you, Daddy, Daisy, and our family.

Heartbreak will never be easy. But remember, on your toughest of days, that you never know when the universe is preparing to send you someone special.

I love you more than life,
Mama

Breathe

Dear Hartley,

The tension is real. You can feel your jaw clenching, your pulse quickening. Maybe someone at work has said something horrible to you. Or you just found out that you've been lied to. Or you're drowning in a sea of responsibilities and completely overwhelmed. All of these things lead to one common result—stress. Fortunately, there is something simple you can do that will help you feel better.

Breathe.

Sure, we breathe naturally. But there is also the practice of focused, intentional breathing that can help you in so many ways. Conscious breathing sends a signal through your body to calm down, stimulates a wave of relaxation through your muscles and organs, and reduces the stress that builds up throughout the day. By taking the time every day to focus on your breathing, you can increase the endorphins that make you feel more up than down, stimulate your lymphatic system to detoxify your body, relieve pain, improve digestion, and empower your body to regenerate and heal.

It's so rewarding, Hartley. And although it seems really simple, focused breathing can be pretty challenging at first. It's kind of like sitting still. When you're used to constant motion, juggling a zillion tasks all the time like we often do, sitting still feels really odd. At least at first. Same goes for paying attention to your breath. At first, it will seem silly, foreign, and maybe even a little uncomfortable. But if you stick with it, your body will thank you, and you will feel the effects of those stress releases everywhere.

Mama isn't the best candidate for things like focused breathing and meditation. As you may already know a bit by now, my mind tends to be of the racing kind. It's a genuine challenge for me to quiet my thinking and just breathe. I started meditating during the COVID pandemic because my brain was getting filled with so much serious, often-devastating news. Deep breathing, sitting still, and clearing my mind for a few minutes a day helped me enormously. The sounds of water, especially rain or ocean waves, also help me relax, so I'll often play those while meditating. I'm still not an expert on any of this by any stretch of the imagination, but I've come a long way, and I look forward to those quiet times when my mind can take a break.

I've also found that I can turn to my breathing when life hands me a sack of lemons and expects me to quickly make lemonade. When I'm sad or filled with worry, finding my breath reminds me of my inner strength and gets my priorities back where they need to be.

Try to find the calm in your body and your mind, Hartley. When the world or the room you're in is filled with gloomy chaos, take a break, step outside into nature if you can, and just breathe. If you can't be outside, that's okay too. Find a quiet place to close your eyes and give your mind a small reset, a chance to nourish itself.

Even on the days that feel wonderful, when you hear great news, eat delicious food, and see good people, still take those few minutes to be still and let your mind rest. That tiny window of detoxification and stress release will help your body cope with a potentially not-so-wonderful day ahead.

Your body is an amazing machine. It wants to work with you and for you, but sometimes it needs your help. It needs you to take a few moments of total peace to let it regenerate and clean out the waste materials that will only make you feel sick, stressed, and much less happy. I hope you learn this lesson sooner than I did.

There is so much to gain by taking a pause and letting yourself breathe.

I love you more than life,
Mama

Two Beautiful Words

Dear Hartley,

I'm not great at some things. Like relaxing, for example. That takes real effort on my part. But one thing I've always been good at is stepping up to say, "I'm sorry."

We all make mistakes. We all have character flaws, weak moments when we do or say something that hurts someone else. We may get angry and intentionally spew something nasty that we soon regret. Sometimes, in the course of an argument, we say things we don't even mean. We may say things that are self-absorbed or poor reflections of who we are, who we want to be, and what we want to put out there into the world. It's embarrassing and frustrating, but it happens to all of us.

The tricky part is that once we say something mean to someone, it's too late to take it back. It's out there in the universe, in the air, in the space between you and someone else. The words have been heard, felt, and someone's feelings about what you've said are now involved. They may get sad, hurt, angry, or any combination of those emotions. There's a chance they'll even say something horrible right back to you, in which case you could end up stuck in a revolving cycle of bad words with them.

You can't take it back, but you can try to fix it.

The first step toward doing that is to say, "I'm sorry."

Saying "I'm sorry" is an acknowledgment to yourself and to others that you did something wrong, that you don't feel good about what you said or did, and that you are aware that it didn't feel good for someone else to be on the receiving end of your words or actions. It's owning up to your mistakes, saying that "Yes, I messed up and I'm sorry if my behavior caused you pain."

"I'm sorry" forces you to sit with the pain you caused someone else, feel a sense of disappointment in yourself, and be inspired to do better next time, to be a better person to the people around you. It helps the person you hurt to feel heard and important to you. It can go a long way in rebuilding an important relationship.

Both sides of the "I'm sorry" equation are important. If someone makes a mistake, hurts you, and sincerely apologizes, there is kindness and humanity in forgiveness, in giving that person a chance to do better.

Of course, a genuine "I'm sorry" should be followed by a positive change in behavior. I'm certainly not suggesting that it's wise to be a doormat for someone repeatedly doing or saying terrible things to you, apologizing, and then doing and saying terrible things to you again and again. Patterns of behavior like that aren't healthy, and there are relationships that need to be ended and peacefully walked away from when you know they're simply not good for you. Apologies that are consistently followed by the same bad behavior are what we call fake apologies.

What I'm talking about are sincere apologies, followed by

constructive changes in behavior and a commitment to do better. That's not to say we'll never make the same mistake twice, but you'll be able to tell the difference between someone who's making positive changes and someone who's not. When someone apologizes to you, think about the person apologizing and whether or not you feel the apology is sincere. Think about their behavior. Consider whether you're ready to offer forgiveness as a way to heal wounds and if that feels right.

Ultimately, only you will be able to make these big decisions about apologizing and forgiving. Only you can determine who you'd like to continue to walk through life with, be it a friend, partner, or family member. I will say, though, that there's something about forgiving someone, even if you no longer choose to have them in your life, that lifts a weight off of *you* and helps you to walk through the world a little lighter and brighter.

Daddy and I don't really have big fights, mostly because Daddy is so wired for calm that he calms me in even my most un-calm moments. But of course, like any couple, we've had our disagreements. When you were super tiny and not sleeping, Daddy and I were completely sleep-deprived. Every now and then, exhaustion made us say something not so nice to each other. We would catch ourselves right away, or almost right away, and apologize, knowing full well that our exhaustion was getting the best of us. I'm very lucky that your daddy is great about saying "I'm sorry" and owning up when he does or says something he wishes he hadn't.

I wasn't always so lucky. The guy I dated the year before I met your daddy didn't quite have the "I'm sorry" chip. He wouldn't admit he had ever done anything wrong, let alone apologize. I have no idea if he felt bad about the stuff he did—the lying, the cheating, the lying again. Maybe he did feel bad and just couldn't bring himself to say

"I'm sorry," for fear that he would then have to face what he'd done. Even though there's nothing he could've said by the end to make me stay in that relationship, the apology would've meant something to me. We had been friends before we dated, and had shared a lot of laughs and family stories. I wanted to believe that despite everything, all of that had meant something to him, that I had meant something to him. I walked away feeling like I hadn't, and that stunk.

Two simple words would've made a big difference.

I hope you grow to understand why it's so important to say "I'm sorry" and to have it said to you. I hope you grow to feel that the "I'm sorry" you say can help *you* as much as the person you say it to.

I can help teach you that, but the way you treat people when you're all grown up will be up to you. Kindness and accountability go really, really far, Hartley. They go far in mending fences and helping you feel like you're learning and becoming a better person day to day.

Never forget that the energy you put out into the world matters. The universe, the world around you, they receive that energy and hear your "I'm sorry" too. They respond to it in some way, with energy of their own. That energy exchange has the power to spread far and wide.

Imagine if each of us took a little time to realize the value of our words, actions, and apologies, and what they all mean to one another and the world around us.

I hope that you and your generation will appreciate the value of accountability and forgiveness more than ours did, and that because of that, the world will be a better place.

I love you more than life,
Mama

Celery Juice

Dear Hartley,

Celery juicing is part of our morning, every morning. It has made a big difference in how I feel, and I hope it will always be something that kick-starts your day. When Mama starts taking celery out of the fridge, you run over to the juicer and wait for a cup. You even start pointing and smiling as the fresh juice comes through.

Since you love your celery juice so much, I thought it might be important to ensure that you have, in writing, the very complex process involved in making it:

1. Purchase organic celery bunches. Pick ones that don't look wilted.
2. Cut off the very tops and very bottoms.
3. Wash them well. If you have a filter option on your sink, use that water.
4. Use a peeler to remove any yucky stuff that doesn't wash off.
5. Place the wet celery on paper towels while you set up the juicer.
6. Hit the start button on the juicer.

7. Push each celery stalk through.
8. Pour the wonderful green concoction into a glass.
9. Drink.
10. Clean the juicer so it's ready for tomorrow.

I hope that covers it.

Enjoy it before breakfast every morning, right after a tall glass of water with lemon to start your day.

I love you more than life,
Mama

Mindset Reset

Dear Hartley,

When I need to recharge my soul, or just need a minute of total mindless peace, I watch *Beverly Hills 90210* reruns. I was going to say that you may not even know what *90210* is, but then I realized that of course you do because I watched the whole series (again) while pregnant with you. On a few occasions since you were born, the *90210* theme song has come on, and you stop whatever you're doing to stare at the TV. I'm pretty sure you already know Dylan, Brenda, Kelly, and the crew all too well.

My point here is not that we all need to immerse ourselves in '90s teenage dramas. It's that we all have that thing, that activity, that escape which clears our mind and improves our outlook on just about everything. I have several, actually. Exercise. Pushing you on a swing at the playground. Time in the sunshine with Daddy. A green juice. And, of course, an occasional trip down the college hallways of *Felicity*, or to Capeside with the *Dawson's Creek* gang, or to the Walsh house on *90210*. Those '90s TV shows remind me of a really special time in my life, and sometimes revisiting them helps me recapture that energy.

I hope you can always find that thing or those things that recharge you. Make space for them, whatever they are. Some days it might seem impossible to make that space. Whether it's working out, starting a fun project, or learning a new skill, you may feel that there's no space for any of it. And maybe you'll even have an excuse or two: *There's no room to work out, I have no time for a fun project, I don't have the energy to learn something new.* Try to change your mindset in those moments. Changing your mindset can help you see that you can make plenty of space for the things that will help you recharge.

You can recharge your body and soul in a small corner of your living room. As I write this, I'm gearing up to do a workout downstairs on your foam mats while you sleep. You should've seen the tiny space in our old apartment where I exercised when COVID struck and all of the gyms shut down. It was a little corner next to the bed.

Change the way you look at a room, and the room changes.

You can also shift how you use the hours in a day to make space for your priorities. It's amazing how much time you can save if you stick your phone in a charging station and ignore it for a while.

Always make space for the things that make you happy. Whether it's a walk in the park, a good movie, a workout, cooking dinner, dancing, having a long conversation with a good friend—let those things fill up your soul and your life.

Remember, your mindset is in charge. It makes space for whatever you want and need. And if something you don't want and don't need has to get pushed aside to make that space, then start pushing.

It's all up to you.

I love you more than life,
Mama

Pulling a Bila

Dear Hartley,

One night around nine o'clock, we were taping a segment on the show *Red Eye* related to *Star Wars*. I can't remember exactly what the segment was about, but I do remember that I had told everyone in advance that I knew almost nothing about *Star Wars*.

"That'll make it funnier," the producer said.

She wound up being right.

What I recall is that somewhere in the midst of our on-air discussion, I tried to make a point about Dark Vader. Yep, I said *Dark Vader*.

I think that may have also been the night I called lightsabers...wait for it...*lifesavers*. Although it's possible I made that blunder on another evening.

Before you rush to my defense and think, *Well, Mom, everyone spits out the wrong word by mistake when talking sometimes*, let me be straight up with you and say that your mama really did think Dark Vader was the character and his weapon was a lifesaver.

We laughed a lot on the set that night about what I had said. *Red Eye* was a great place to make fun of yourself, and I loved that.

Hartley, you'll come to know that I, like many, have my own brand of silliness. I sometimes say really silly things, and then we all laugh about them together. Or I'll do something really silly, and we'll laugh about that. I now call it "Pulling a Bila." Your grandma doesn't love that slogan, as she's also a Bila and doesn't do the silly stuff I do, but she's come around to laughing when I use the expression. I got my "Pulling a Bila" idea from a *Friends* episode, "The One with the 'Cuffs." In that episode, Monica's fake blue nail falls into the quiche she's been preparing for her mother's dinner party, and her mother is ready with a frozen lasagna contingency plan because she knew her daughter might "pull a Monica." For the record, I don't wear fake nails, but I can totally see myself wrecking a quiche in some other horrific way.

I Pulled a Bila just this morning. I was driving to an appointment on Long Island. It was raining slightly, though I could see just fine. Nonetheless, I drove right into a pothole the size of a kiddie pool on the highway. I heard a *BOOM!*, then saw the "low tire pressure" symbol on the dashboard. Next thing I knew, I was driving a little lopsided. Then I smelled burning rubber. *That can't be good*, I thought. Shaking my head, I did what any rational person would do. I drove for a bit on what I'd later see was a majorly blown-out tire, until I could find a suitable place to pull over. And by suitable, I mean a spot where I could purchase a green juice.

Green juice helps everything. Even flat tires.

I called Daddy.

"Why are you laughing?" he said.

"You're not going to believe this."

Oh, he believed it all right.

What wasn't to believe? It was me, his number one goofball.

I had Pulled a Bila yet again.

Daddy called the dealership where we had leased the car and they told us that our damaged tire could be driven on for fifty miles as long as I stayed under fifty miles per hour. Daddy found a service station for me to take the car to that was right by my appointment, and I was able to get the tire replaced within a few hours.

You may be wondering why I didn't just change the tire myself. Remember that letter (see "Desert Island Dude") I wrote to you about real-life skill sets and why they're important? Learn how to change a tire, Hartley. Your mama, of course, did not know. At one point, your daddy mentioned something about a car jack, and I made a joke about a jack-in-the-box, and that's pretty much how that part of the conversation went down.

I did learn how to change a tire when I got home, though. Sort of. Almost. It's a work in progress.

The whole tire fiasco was super annoying, yes, but it was also a reason to feel grateful. Grateful that I was okay and hadn't gotten hurt in the whole ordeal. Grateful that I had the money to replace the tire, which may not have been the case at other times in my life, when money was tighter. Grateful that your daddy and I could make fun of me for Pulling a Bila. Grateful that we could laugh about it all, like we do about so many things.

Making fun of myself has been a solid part of my health care regimen for years. We feel good when we laugh, and it's not just me who thinks our minds and bodies are better for it. Studies show that laughing, like intentional breathing, releases positive, happy-feeling endorphins into the body, decreases stress hormones, and boosts our immune systems.

It's a simple prescription: Laugh. It helps heal your body and your mind.

Laughter can also pivot you away from anger in times of distress. Whenever I start getting upset or super stressed out, I turn to Daddy and say, "Make me laugh." He does, and it immediately improves my mood.

I've known too many people who have a great sense of humor about everything but themselves. I dated someone for a short time who was funny as all heck, but could not laugh at himself. Ever. Any joke directed at him in even the slightest way would completely offend him. It was a terrible match for me, as you might imagine. It also made me incredibly sad because I knew that if he could've laughed at himself, it would've helped him through so many of life's challenging moments.

Hartley, there is no one on this earth who doesn't do something silly now and then. Some of us do it more than others. You'll do it too. It's so important that you're able to get a kick out of your silly moments. Those moments are human, they're real, and they're endearing because they're human and real.

Yes, life is a serious proposition. I want you to have serious moments, and you will. But serious can be draining. It can be exhausting. Laughing at yourself when you do ridiculous things, and laughing in general, can be such a welcome break from all of that seriousness. And remember, laughter is contagious. It can shift the mood of the room you're in, the mood of your day, the mood of your life. The same goes for smiling. I remember a TV producer once giving me a note to "smile less." That was terrible advice. Smile more, Hartley. Always smile more.

Fortunately, you're a goofball already. You laugh at almost everything silly that we do. Mama knocks things over by mistake all the time, and you chuckle. Soon enough, we're all laughing hysterically. You love my silly noises, Daddy's silly game where he chases you on all fours, and the moonwalk I do when I'm overtired. My "Thriller" dance is a big hit too. You make funny faces and then laugh like crazy when I imitate them. You're basically a goofball born to two goofball parents.

Daddy and I had been goofing around for a few years before you got here. I remember one night all too well, the night your daddy and I went to the Daytime Emmy Awards in Los Angeles. My co-hosts and I had been nominated during my time on *The View*. It meant a lot to me to get that Emmy nomination because when I was a kid, I used to watch the Daytime Emmys on TV with my grandma. Being on that red carpet years later really meant something to me. It took me back to my childhood and reminded me of my grandma's smile. She would've gotten a real kick out of me being there.

What I remember most about that night, though, was that Daddy and I decided to skip the parties that followed the ceremony. As you'll come to see, I'm not the most social of social beings. While others in my industry were networking and sharing contact information, your daddy and I, still in our black-tie garb, grabbed takeout food and ate it on the hood of the car while parked at a gorgeous scenic overlook, then took a long Southern California drive. We cracked jokes for hours. I remember that the zipper on my dress popped off because we had eaten so many tacos, and I loved that. We laughed and laughed and laughed.

It had been kind of a life-changing, eye-opening, knock-your-socks-off year, and certainly not one of my easiest. I had been on a hit show and then, all of a sudden, I wasn't. But I remember thinking that night in the car with your daddy, driving around Pasadena in my fancy dress, feet bare and tummy full, how happy I was that we were able to find so much laughter in it all.

As you'll find out, life is a series of twists and turns. Sometimes it's not easy to find the laughter. But you have to. You must. I hope with my whole heart that you always do.

Your daddy and I always find the silly in tough days. You're a part of that now. Your laughter has already taught me so much. I'm a clean freak at heart, but you've shown me how to lie down in messy, lunch-stained clothes, amid a scattered pile of toys, and just laugh.

Hartley, I'm grateful for the good in this world—the honest, the kind, the sincere, and the true. And when it comes to the not-so-good things that we all encounter, don't forget to just keep laughing. It's the best medicine for dealing with almost anything.

Especially when you've Pulled a Bila.

I love you more than life,
Mama

You, the Architect

Dear Hartley,

In my dreams, you're laughing. You've grown strong. You're a free thinker and fun to be around. You have family and friends who love you as much as you love them. You have a job that's rewarding. You're kind and compassionate. And, of course, you live nearby.

I adore you, Hartley, and want to guarantee you (my version of) the best life ever. But I know that a lot of what your life looks like one day will be up to you. I can provide for you, support you, nurture you, give you as many tools as I can to help you navigate life's obstacles, but only you can create the adult life you want and need. Daddy and I will share our values. We will help you understand laws and rules, determination and discipline, kindness and fairness. We will teach you to respect yourself and others, and we will offer you guidance every step of the way. But eventually, you will be responsible for you. You will have to make the big decisions that will affect the course of your journey.

Each person must be the architect of their own life, Hartley. Create the design, draw the blueprints, oversee the construction. Whatever your life ends up being will be the result of the choices, good and bad, that you made along the way. It will be the product of risks you did and didn't take, doors you shut and others you opened, and yes, how many times you were bold enough to follow your gut.

The power to shape your destiny is yours.

I know that sometimes the thought of having so much control over your life path will seem incredibly empowering. In those moments, you will become idea-driven and goal-focused, making lists and making changes.

At other times, having so much power over your life trajectory will seem incredibly overwhelming. You'll temporarily freeze up and want to sink into a space where your own decisions don't hold so much weight. Let yourself feel those emotions. Let yourself find your way out of them and back toward empowerment. I know that you will.

Our family has always given a loud cheer for resourceful people who care about their families, their communities, and their planet, people who believe in hard work to achieve fulfillment and will defend our collective and individual rights to life, liberty, and the pursuit of happiness.

That's what we hope for you, that you become one of those resourceful people, that you will become the architect of you.

Never be afraid to recognize your own power to create your own happiness. Don't let it burden you—let it be your wings.

I love you more than life,
Mama

Continuing On

Dear Hartley,

Sometimes the end is just the beginning. I guess that's how I feel while writing the final letter of this book.

In these letters, I've talked about topics that I stay up thinking about at night, challenges I've struggled with, hills I've climbed to the top of, only to discover another hill on the other side. In these pages, I've shared a lot of my life, my thoughts, my hopes, and my love.

I love you. You are my biggest and brightest accomplishment.

I worried that I'd get to the end of this book and not want to let it go, not want it to end out of fear that I'd be forgetting to tell you something important before releasing it into the world. I know now, through writing it, that there will always be more I want to share with you, and that's what our life together will be for.

These pages are just the beginning of that sharing. But they're a good beginning, a strong beginning. I hope that they can be a starting point for us to talk about anything and everything.

I remember one of my first dates with your daddy. It was three in the morning before we realized we had been up all night talking. We'd had dinner, then gone for a long walk over the Brooklyn Bridge. We found ourselves on a bench overlooking the East River as the sun came up. We grabbed breakfast at an outdoor café and kept on talking.

The best conversations never end.

I wrote these letters for you, but also for your generation. We're in a complicated time in our country right now. There's a lot of anger and finger-pointing. Some people want to surround themselves with voices who see the world just the way they do. Others want to be around all different kinds of voices saying all different kinds of things, with the hope that we can try to understand one another. I'm part of the latter group.

You've heard the word "conversation" from me many times in these letters. That's because it's everything. It's how we connect, how we figure out who we are, how we grow up, how we fall in love. Without talking to one another, *with* one another, there's nothing. At this moment in time, too many people have forgotten how to listen, and it's impossible to move forward in any good way without that. I wrote in these pages about romance, character, self-discovery, friendship. Conversation is the backbone of all those things and more.

I hope that you and your generation want to hear one another and learn from one another.

As I write this last letter, it's getting dark outside. The bedroom window is open, but it's very quiet, and there's a cool breeze in the air. You're asleep in your crib just a room away, and your baby monitor rests beside me. Every now and then, I'll see you move your little body around, finding a new, more comfortable resting place. I'm thinking about you, what you'll be like when you grow up, what to cook you for lunch tomorrow, and how you'll respond to your very first haircut appointment this week. I can hear Daddy clanking in the kitchen downstairs, likely making a fresh batch of pancake batter for tomorrow's breakfast.

I want you to live a long, beautiful life. And I want you to feel good about it, even the mistakes and the regrets, because they, too, can be part of a wonderful story. I want you to be happy, healthy, to sleep well at night, and to believe that what you're investing your energy in is good for you and good for the world.

If you ever feel lost and are searching for something you can't really define, I hope that you'll revisit these letters. Maybe, just maybe, you'll find it through my words.

I love you more than life.

Always.

Mama

Acknowledgments

So many wonderful people helped me bring this book to life. I'm forever grateful to all of you...

Hartley, my beautiful inspiration, thank you for bringing so much light into my life. Light, purpose, clarity, determination—you have already taught me so much. I love you to the moon and back.

Jeremy, my better half, my partner in crime, my best friend. Writing about our family has brought me so much happiness. Thank you for doing everything you could to give me the time to write my heart out. Thank you for listening when I felt lost. I'm so lucky to get to share my life with you.

Mom and Dad, thank you for your incredible love for me, Jeremy, and Hartley. As a child, I remember feeling so loved. That made all the difference. Thank you, thank you, from the bottom of my heart.

Daisy, my four-pound ball of fur. Thank you for sleeping beside me while I wrote this book, for providing comfort and warmth when my walks down memory lane got tricky. Thank you for being Hartley's best buddy. Mama loves you.

Caroline Sherman, my organizer, my advisor, my friend. Thank you for our heartfelt conversations and for laughing with me until our abs hurt. Thank you for your guidance and for reminding me to follow my inner voice. You're one of the best listeners I know, and that has been an incredible gift to me. I swear, I come up with new projects just so we can work together again. And there will be more. I can't wait for them all.

Brandi Bowles, my literary agent. From our very first conversation, I walked away thinking, "This is a woman who gets things done." And you do, and you have. Thank you for your passion for this project. I'm honored to have you on my team.

Lia Aponte, my television agent. What a year, my dear friend. Thank you for always believing in me and having my back through the sunshine and the storms. I love you like family.

Daisy Hutton, my publisher. You embraced this book idea with so much heart right from the beginning. Thank you for inviting me to share my voice, my family, and my hopes and dreams with the world.

Alex Pappas, my editorial director. You've been so supportive and kind throughout this book's journey, and I'm so grateful for your feedback and hard work.

Abigail Skinner, my editorial assistant. Thank you for your positive energy and commitment. They mean so much.

Kristen Andrews, my creative director. Thank you for your excitement about this book's cover and all of your artistic input. I'm so appreciative of your creative vision.

Katie Robison, senior publicist at Hachette. Thank you for your tireless dedication to getting this book and its message out there. You've been so amazing to collaborate with.

Patsy Jones, VP of marketing at Hachette. Thank you for managing this book's rollout brilliantly, and for your organization and thoughtful ideas.

Carolyn Kurek, senior production editor at Hachette. Thank you for overseeing this manuscript with such detail and for your heartfelt support of this book.

To the whole team at Center Street—thank you for believing in me and my words.

Suzanne and Elliot Balaban, my personal publicists. You have been an incredible blessing throughout this process. Thank you for your passion for my book and my goals. Thank you for your warmth and for really listening. I'm so glad I found you.

Jordan Matter, my cover photographer. Also known as my photography magician. I can't imagine anyone else shooting this cover. You've been behind the camera on so many important days for me. Thank you for always bringing your contagious energy and unique vision to our projects. My whole family loves you. You're stuck with us for life, my friend.

Dina Tamburino and Anthony Lee, my hair and makeup book cover team. I'm consistently in awe of your talent. Thank you for bringing so much joy to a day I'll never forget.

To the honest, brave, compassionate, warm souls I've encountered these past few years, thank you. You have inspired me to write, to grow, and to discover the best of what's to come.

About the Author

Jedediah Bila is a mom, wife, daughter, and superhero wannabe. A two-time Emmy Award nominee, she has been a host of ABC's *The View*, Fox News' *Fox & Friends Weekend*, and the Lifetime special *Abby Tells All*. She is the author of *#DoNotDisturb: How I Ghosted My Cell Phone to Take Back My Life* (Harper, 2018). Bila grew up in a small condo on Staten Island with her mom, dad, and cat, Scungilli. She was valedictorian of her class at Wagner College and earned a master of arts in Spanish literature from Columbia University. She also studied at the American Academy of Dramatic Arts in New York City. Bila held a variety of jobs prior to her television career, including teacher and academic dean, marketing associate in the insurance business, and cocktail waitress at a Manhattan lounge with way too many stairs. She currently shares her candid insights across the cultural and political spectrum on television, radio, podcasts, and social media. In her spare time, she reads memoirs, writes her heart out, watches '80s and '90s movies, and dreams about blue oceans and pink sunsets. She currently lives in New York City with her husband, son, and Maltipoo.